PRAISE FOR *A CATECI*

"*A Catechism of the Heart* speaks an openly gay Jesuit priest. This book speaks not only candidly about the hurt, but also about the resiliency and dedication of gay Catholics in the quest to serve their church as ordained priests. I highly recommend it."

—Elisabeth Schüssler Fiorenza,
Krister Stendahl Professor, Harvard University

"One man's painful journey to harmonize sexuality and faith reaches a breaking point, not because of how he is treated by parts of the Roman Catholic Church, but in how church institutions treat other committed and faithful LGBTQ members. This book is insightful, angry, self-deprecating and, at times, very amusing. An original memoir which shows, above all, how one relies on acceptance from others before one can aspire to genuine self-acceptance."

—Mark Dowd, author of *Queer and Catholic*

"Benjamin James Brenkert's book, *A Catechism of the Heart,* is a must-read for those who care about the future and relevance of the church in society. Brenkert is a wise guide as he seeks not to denigrate the church; rather, he helps us all negotiate the healing of controversies in the church and society that so often appear as closed doors to human beings."

—Michael Battle, Herbert Thompson Professor of Church and Society,
General Theological Seminary

"Benjamin James Brenkert's ardent and witty memoir recalls his quest as a member of the Jesuit Society of Jesus to become the first officially ordained 'gay' priest. Challenged by his Catholic family's rejection, he holds on to the all-tolerant Jesus, a man he can love openly, as he navigates between erotic misadventures and spiritual abnegation. Fluctuating between confession and exposé, this memoir draws the curtain on an enigmatic fraternal order, its spiritual and, yes, carnal appetites."

—Barbara Lekatsas, Professor of Comparative Literature, Languages,
and Linguistics, Hofstra University

"Benjamin James Brenkert's new book *A Catechism of the Heart* is a wonderful example of speaking truth to power. To speak truth to power means to demand a moral response to a problem, and that is what Benjamin James Brenkert does in this book. In sharing his experiences in the Jesuits Order as an openly gay man, he does not seek an expedient, easy, or selfish response. Instead, he chooses a God-centeredness approach over the privilege of a Jesuit priesthood, to craft a vision of an LGBTQ liberationist theology—that could faithfully espouse an acceptance and love for LGBTQ people that does not exist in today's Roman Catholic Church."

> —Gerald P. Mallon, Julia Lathrop Professor of Child Welfare, Associate Dean of Scholarship and Research, Silberman School of Social Work, Hunter College

"Ben's story of trying to integrate his conservative faith and his love so that he could be both true to himself and G*d and minister to LGBTQ people, whom his faith rejects, is one that will resonate with many. It is also the story of a deeply patriarchal religious order that tries to maintain its dogma and domination in the face of a changing world. Ben wants to change it from the inside, but the internalized homophobia that he is met with, the privileges that the order has, belies their focus on social justice for the poor and the marginalized. These contradictions he can no longer overlook when the church starts to fire their loyal LGBTQ employees, because his silence would make him complicit."

> —J. A. Myers, author of *The Good Citizen: The Markers of Privilege in America,* Associate Professor of Political Science, Director of Public Administration Concentration, Marist College

"Through all the bracing honesty of this moving memoir—its searing exposure of the homophobia of Roman Catholic teaching—the most impressive aspect of this book is the sheer spirituality of Brenkert. His confession reveals a closeness to God and Jesus that is breathtaking. I found myself moved to jealousy by his love for God and desire for Jesus. In pain, irresistible love."

> —Dale B. Martin, Woolsey Professor Emeritus of Religious Studies, Yale University, and author of *Sex and the Single Savior*

"Brenkert's confession is a story of faith, family, and freedom told with sincerity, sensitivity, and an uncensored memory. It is also the story of a generation coming to terms with sexuality in ways that would force historical changes in the structures of social norms. This song of self is beautifully told, inviting the reader to share a journey of blindness and insight, guided by a search for personal awareness and unwavering commitment to love."

> —Greg Moses, Philosophy Lecturer, Texas State University

A Catechism of the Heart

A Catechism of the Heart

A Jesuit Missioned to the Laity

BENJAMIN JAMES BRENKERT

foreword by Robert Waldron

RESOURCE *Publications* · Eugene, Oregon

A CATECHISM OF THE HEART
A Jesuit Missioned to the Laity

Resource Publications
An Imprint of Wipf and Stock Publishers
199 W. 8th Ave., Suite 3
Eugene, OR 97401

www.wipfandstock.com

PAPERBACK ISBN: 978-1-7252-7444-0
HARDCOVER ISBN: 978-1-7252-7445-7
EBOOK ISBN: 978-1-7252-7446-4

Manufactured in the U.S.A.   07/07/20

Dedicated in loving memory
to my dad, Albert and to my mom, Loretta.
With gratitude and thanksgiving for their love, strength and support.

Take action, the responsibility is yours . . . be strong and do it.

—Ezra 10:4

And on this journey something happened to him which it will be good to have written, so that people can understand how Our Lord used to deal with this soul: a soul that was still blind, though with great desires to serve him as far as its knowledge went. . .And so, when he would make up his mind to do some penance that the saints did, his aim was to do the same, and more besides. And in these thoughts he had all his consolation, not considering anything within himself, nor knowing what humility was, or charity, or patience, or discernment in regulating and balancing these virtues. Rather, his whole purpose was to do these great exterior deeds because so the saints had done them for the glory of God, without considering any other more individual circumstance.

—*The Autobiography of St. Ignatius of Loyola*

On the contrary, those who are deprived of love are the most demanding and discriminating in what they will receive. A child hungry for love is most quick to detect and reject condescension, bribery or manipulation when it masquerades as love, and requires most full assurance of the authenticity of that which is offered to him. Though he has never tasted authentic love, he knows already the taste of what he needs.

—W. H. Vanstone

When I meet a gay person, I have to distinguish between his being gay and being part of a lobby. If they accept the Lord and have goodwill, who am I to judge them? They shouldn't be marginalized. The tendency is not the problem. They're our brothers.

—Pope Francis I

A century ago, anyone would have thought it absurd to talk about homosexual marriage. Today those who oppose it are excommunicated from society. . .The fear of this spiritual power of the Antichrist is then only more than natural, and it really needs the help of prayers on the part of an entire diocese and of the Universal Church in order to resist it.

—Pope Emeritus Benedict XVI

Contents

Foreword

A Catechism of the Heart: A Jesuit Missioned to the Laity is a riveting memoir of a young man with a dream: to become a Jesuit priest. He was a faithful, pious Catholic, matriculated at a Catholic college and lived by the teachings of the Gospel and the Catholic church. He read biographies of St. Ignatius of Loyola and carefully studied the Saint's *Spiritual Exercises*, embracing their lessons of discernment and wisdom. But there is one problem: he had magnified his dream: he not only wanted to become a Jesuit priest, but also to become the first openly gay ordained Jesuit priest in the world.

Our author had never hidden his sexuality from the Jesuits. When they accepted him into the Society of Jesus, they knew he was gay because he was completely transparent and informed his Jesuit superiors. And because he passed the strict Jesuitical vetting, our author began to believe, because they accepted him into the Jesuit order, that it was not far-fetched for him, after almost a decade of Jesuit study, to believe that he would become the first openly gay ordained Jesuit priest in the world.

As he approached ordination, another narrative emerged. The Jesuit order relayed to our author that his becoming an ordained gay priest would not happen, for the church does not accept homosexuality, describing it in the Catholic catechism as an intrinsically disordered and morally culpable condition. He begged his superiors to allow his ordination, and they consented to it but not as an openly gay priest. His gayness (by the vow of Obedience) would have to remain a secret that only his Jesuit order and he would know. He was hurt by this rejection because he believed that he had been accepted as a gay man. He was further hurt because there are many Jesuit priests who are gay, all known to each other, a sort of secret subculture of gay priests, who are parish priests, teachers, professors and theologians. In his protestation, he received no support from them, and he felt egregiously betrayed.

Then arrived the final blow: nationwide the church summarily fired Catholic gay employees and volunteers. And here he was on the verge of becoming a Jesuit priest. No one was firing him. He was about to be or-dained and likely assigned to a parish or a college to teach. He would actu-ally be a gay ordained priest, but no one would know about it.

Ironically, during this tumultuous time, Jesuit Pope Francis I had raised the hopes of Catholic gays around the world with a seemingly nonjudgmen-tal stance, saying about gays and their lifestyle, "Who am I to judge?" But since then he has seemingly had a change of heart.

Finally, to be true to himself, our author decided to leave the Jesuits. It was the most difficult decision of his life because he loved being a Jesuit and following in the steps of St. Ignatius Loyola. His family urged him not to throw away about nearly ten years of Jesuit living and study. But his conscience would not allow him to remain a Jesuit. He then vowed to serve his gay community by telling the world his story: all eloquently captured in *A Catechism of the Heart: A Jesuit Missioned to the Laity* .

ROBERT WALDRON

Preface

Dear Readers,

As I settled into my new apartment, decorating with excitement, a new friend asked me, Why do you have such beautiful Christian art? These crucifixes and Madonnas bely the point: The Church rejects gays and you are a gay man.

I answered my friend, the God who loves me is not the sole property of a Church that rejects people like me, LGBTQ people. That god would be too small, a god not worth praying to. I continued, homosexuality is part of God's creation. Such is the conversation between two gays in May 2020.

While writing this memoir, and with the exception of writing about my loving family, I disguised some real names to protect others' privacy. I went out of my way to care for, and to conceal the identities of the people I knew and lived with. It is my memoir, my story. Many of the personal letters and essays referenced here were composed while in the Society of Jesus, and remain part of my Jesuit file, tucked away in a Province office. Other writings, like my retreat diaries I have kept and protected from wear and tear.

My hope is that this memoir will present readers with an opportunity to affirm their true selves in the eyes of their God or no God at all, and if they are Roman Catholic, an opportunity to know thyself and to make an election (the Ignatian Spirituality term for making a change/decision following a discernment) like me and to dare to leave the Church of one's youth for another that is fully affirming—one that does not couch acceptance on reconciliation and celibacy.

I want to emphasize the purpose of my memoir. It is a spiritual contemplation about an old hope: to become a gay ordained Roman Catholic priest, to
serve God's children and to freely respond to God's calling.

When the Church fired gay and lesbian employees and volunteers, I said,
Enough! Firing people for who they love does not make sense. Jesus drew
people to himself, to come and see, to put on that *sensus Christi*. Fr. Pedro
Arrupe, S.J., the 28th Superior General of the Society of Jesus prayed for
collaboration with Christ, Give me that *sensus Christi* that I may feel with
your feelings, with the sentiments of your heart, which basically are love for
your Father and love for all men and women.

My memoir underscores the reasons why I left the Jesuits. I could not, in
good conscience, be a priest, Jesuit or otherwise, while remaining in the
closet. That is not the making of a happy priesthood.

I end in gratitude. I thank you for accompanying me on this pilgrimage, and
for reading my story about being a son of Ignatius of Loyola. For in turn,
taking action that all may be loved, for God is love itself.

All for the greater glory of God.

BENJAMIN JAMES BRENKERT

Introduction

THE SOCIETY OF JESUS is an international Roman Catholic religious order of priests and brothers. Some estimate the Society of Jesus to include 10,000 men worldwide. The Jesuits have been the confessors of kings, the spiritual directors to popes; they also run a network of educational institutions that rivals the Ivy League. While fewer and fewer Jesuits may work in the trenches with the poor, the order still has access to a vast network of the rich and powerful, men and women who help shape Church policy, who steward schools and institutions with their time, talent and treasure. Men and women, people of faith and no faith at all, straight and gay people steward the Society of Jesus. These people collaborate with the Jesuits to improve the lives of the world's materially and spiritually poor. Such is the Jesuit "Brand"!

For just about 10 years I was a gay, mostly celibate Jesuit Scholastic, a member of the Society of Jesus in good standing. I chose to leave the Society of Jesus over the firing of gay and lesbian employees and volunteers, such an un-Christian policy has severely immoral consequences: it treats peoples as means when they are ends in themselves. It fragments the whole LGBTQ person, telling the LGBTQ person that the part of you that is not heterosexual is not holy, that it is moral to be sexuality-blind (to not see LGBTQ for who God made them to be) and "righteous" to call LGBTQ to forgiveness and reconciliation when they love a person of the same-sex. Imagine the negative consequences of such a tradition: shame, resentment, and second-class citizenship. Its absurd to say that LGBTQ people want special treatment, that gay rights are special rights, such language is homophobic whether it is blatantly obvious (AKA the Church of Pope Emeritus Benedict XVIS) or inconspicuously ambiguous (AKA the Church of Pope Francis I). Such a policy thwarts human flourishing of some of the most marginalized members of our society.

My years as a Jesuit were profoundly joyful; at the same time, I entered a hidden religious and spiritual world that many know little about. In many ways, as I left the Society of Jesus my heart was broken, and I was also angry.

My decision to write a memoir about those years is not done to hurt anyone. It is to the truth about my years as a Jesuit, an order that in the end rejected me because I am a gay man who refuses to hide in a closet. My desiring to be an openly gay Jesuit priest was one that frightened my Jesuit superiors, many of whom are gay themselves.

Today, the Society of Jesus and her stewards are now at a pivotal moment in history: A time when Pope Francis I has taken the Jesuit "Brand" global, when more and more men, women and young people are coming out as members of the LGBTQ community, when more and more families and friends know LGBTQ people. Around the world, they are reaching out to the Roman Catholic Church to turn to the Gospel of Jesus Christ, to teach the world about God's love and mercy, and about the need for mutual respect, human relationship and the dignity and worth of all human beings; the Church hierarchy has long entrusted such a mission to the Jesuits. No other religious order possesses the talent, time or treasure to fulfill this mission. Furthermore, no religious order is trusted and respected like the Society of Jesus.

It is the Society of Jesus who puts these three questions on the minds and hearts of men and women: What have I done for Christ?, What am I doing for Christ? and What ought I do for Christ? The Jesuits are holy men, historically trailblazers, men called to serve God with total love and total service (Spanish translation: *en todo amar y servir*).

St. Ignatius of Loyola (1491–1556), the youngest son in a noble Basque family, was trained as a page at the court of Castile. He was wounded at the siege of Pamplona (1521). While convalescing from an injury, he underwent a deep conversion experience. He retired for a year of reflection at Manresa; the notes he jotted down at that time formed the basis of his influential spiritual guidebook, *The Spiritual Exercises*. After a treacherous pilgrimage to Jerusalem, he undertook prolonged studies (mainly in Paris), gradually attracting like-minded students, like Saints Peter Faber and Francis Xavier. They took "vows" in 1534, from 1540, when Ignatius was elected Superior General, he lived in Rome organizing, largely through a series of letters, the astonishing spread of the Jesuits. He was canonized, along with Saints Francis Xavier, and Teresa of Avila in 1622.

At a chapel at La Storta, Italy, where Ignatius and his first companions, Fathers Peter Faber and James Lainez, had stopped to pray, God the Father revealed to him, "I will be favorable to you in Rome" and that he would place him (Ignatius) with His Son. Ignatius did not know what his experience meant, for it could have meant persecution as well as success since Jesus experienced both. Still, Ignatius sought humility not conceit. It is this same *risen* Jesus who is now inviting the Society of Jesus and her stewards to serve the least and most marginalized amongst us, among these include LGBTQ people. Father David Fleming, one of my favorite Jesuits, now deceased, once told a group of young Jesuits in formation about how we should follow Jesus,

> Jesus *carrying his cross* indicates to us that we will find the cross of disappointment, darkness, diminishment, and sorrow and pain in the ordinary love moments of prayer and community and in the service moments of mission and ministry. Remember that the world we see in Ignatius' *Contemplation on Love* is one in which we pray for the grace to be able to love and serve in all things, *en todo amar y servir*. That is how we follow the risen Jesus carrying his cross.

Growing up as a gay Catholic, I can say that I was with Jesus even in my suffering; that I was with Jesus during my own disappointment, darkness and diminishment in the face of rejection by my family and Church. Yet, I can only use conjecture to suspect that knowing a priest, like David Fleming, would have made a difference in my life. What if priests could publicly identify their sexuality? No, the 1980s and 1990s were a time when the Roman Catholic Church on Long Island had a great impact on me; before long I sought to serve God as a Roman Catholic Jesuit priest, *all for the Greater Glory of God.*

The present moment is a time of gay ascendancy, the Church finds this truth inconvenient, and her ethics remain incoherent; in response to the secular world's embrace of same-sex marriage the Church tells the world it is failing humanity. How incongruent is the relationship between the Church hierarchy and her laity? No matter what any churchman says, gays are just not accepted, they are men with an "orientation" toward same-sex desire and same-sex intimacy, they are not "natural," having as Pope Emeritus Benedict XVI said, "a more or less strong tendency ordered toward an intrinsic moral evil; thus the inclination itself must be seen as an objective disorder." He also said that same-sex marriage is an "anarchic" form of "pseudo-matrimony." But, being gay is *not* a choice! Gay youth and gay men still face societal stigma, violence and discrimination remain possibilities for them, whether one lives in the West or the East, in cities like Philadelphia and St. Petersburg or the West Bank. The presence of gay men in the priesthood is paradoxical.

In truth, the Church does not want gay men to apply for the priesthood. But, of course, there are religious orders who ignore such contrivances; for me this was the promise the Jesuits made to me, at least I thought so. But I'd learn over time that the Jesuit "commitment to social justice," which differentiates their priests and brothers from the more well known diocesan Roman Catholic priests, is not necessarily valid or reliable. Still, diocesan priests are not necessarily agents for social change, and many do not see them as social activists. As a small boy, the priests in the Church of the Blessed Sacrament enkindled in me a desire to be in relationship with Jesus, one that I still actively pursue as an adult.

Chapter 1

To Question Searchingly

I GREW UP IN a yellow, Tudor-style home in Valley Stream, New York. Just east of Queens. The town is full of middle-class families, who seek the benefits of Long Island with its beaches, malls and suburban benefits, like cleaner air and greater space. Growing up Benjamin James Brenkert, a gay Catholic, started here in 1980. I was born to my parents, Albert and Loretta, and joined my siblings William, Anne, Elizabeth and Catharine. When I was born, my parents were in their forties and fifties, and my oldest sibling sixteen and my youngest eight. Ours was a Roman Catholic family more than it was German, Italian or Polish. And, of course, we were a thoroughly American family. As Brenkerts, our traditions, our way of life, our thought processes were shaped by the Christian religion that for millennia had influenced, if not created, the modern world and Western civilization.

My dad was a New York City Fire Department (FDNY) fire inspector, and my mom worked for Nassau Downs Off-Track Betting (OTB). My dad never went to college, and my mom spent a year or two taking courses, but left to raise a family. In many ways, because of the age gaps, I grew up as an only child, with 3 sister-moms, who each took turns "nannying" me while I went from diapers, to walking, to talking, to thinking, and to school.

My siblings have a very different understanding of life at home than I do; they heard, saw and felt things differently from me. Still, today, when we talk about our home on Fir Street, it's as if I am the one experiencing life through the lens of magical realism, while they are less modern, much more conservative, and much more protective of what they saw as the "good" times.

My earliest memory of my dad sees him coming home from work in his FDNY uniform; he is a strikingly handsome man, whose features include blonde hair and blue eyes. He stands at 5 feet 10 inches tall, but to my young eyes, he looks larger than life. He is smoking his favorite cigarette, a Parliament. He doesn't speak much, but his eyes say that he wants to but cannot, as if something is holding him back, preventing him from experiencing, perhaps enjoying, the world. If I could have surmised then that it was fear, well, perhaps my dad would have made more sense to me, but what does any four year old know about manic depression or alcoholism, or how these two illnesses, when co-occurring, affect one person or a person's family system?

My dad also had a tic, not a verbal or physical tic. It was the sound of air passing through his lips, and he could not stop ticking. He'd tick after every word. All of my life I'd hated this strange, if not abnormal, noise. It haunted me, and I felt embarrassed by it, unsure of it or how it came to be, for after all, no other adult or child I'd ever met made such a sound. As I grew up, I'd imitate it, not in mockery but because a son copies his father. Later, I asked my mom, "What caused dad's tick?" I also asked, perhaps just as often, "When did his sadness begin?" And as the years progressed, I looked for answers in my dad's dresser drawers or his workbench in the basement, the places where he kept mementos, and I looked there when my dad sat watching TV, drinking his beer, or doing some other errand, like delivering meals on wheels to the elderly, his concern for and generosity towards others so typical of him. I wanted to know my dad: as I said, he was to me larger than life, often funny, but also so withdrawn, so introspective, so voiceless that it made me feel uncertain, if not anxious. He was an alcoholic, a Jekyll and Hyde, a victim of rage and a troubled childhood; he was sometimes verbally abusive, transforming him into a frightening figure.

My mom was the oldest child born to an Italian-American dad and a Polish-immigrant mom. She was a brown-eyed beauty and loving and spiritual. I remember her reading the Bible to me at bedtime, stories from the Book of Genesis, and her tucking me into bed. Mom worked often to help support our family, and so my sister-moms were in charge of me, which, in a sense, means that they were also raising me; consequently, they were a great influence on my life. With four "moms," I, therefore, cannot describe myself as free. But no sister-mom can replace a child's natural desire to attach to his or her mom. My mom rarely expressed affection physically. Looking back on this, I can see why, even as an adult, I sought to hug and to kiss her and make up for what I missed as a youth.

My parents grew up on the same street in Maspeth, Queens, and since my mom's mom was alive, a Polish immigrant, we would drive to visit her just as often as we could. Katharine Gallo was the warmest woman I knew;

her eyes sparkled, and she made the most delicious stuffed cabbage a boy could ever have. I relished visiting her and sleeping over; we would often go to TSS, a local department store where she'd buy me Transformers (action figures). I'd play in her apartment, or out in the backyard, near the chicken coups. Left to my own devices, I'd of course start looking for things, seeking answers to my dad's tic and sadness, or to why this or that door was closed, or why my grandmother had two twin beds. Every drawer I opened might offer a clue, leading me to some secret knowledge (gnosis) about my dad, but the answers I needed never came, and my dad remained a mystery to me until the very day of his passing in 2010.

By the time I was 6, my brother had left our home, to move in with his fiancé Germaine. My brother had a swimmer's build and was strikingly handsome. I remember finding his Speedos in the room we shared until he moved out. Sixteen years separated us; we were chartered for two different lives. William worked at Toys R' Us, seemed shy and introverted. He'd bully me in ways only a 22-year old brother could; he was by far stronger than me. I remember his coming home from Oneonta State College with a broken ankle. He had tried to water ski, but the waves got the best of him. Once we even visited Mill Pond together, driving there in his Honda Civic, a stick-shift hatchback. As we were walking around the pond, I fell in, and without hesitation, he quickly pulled me out: perhaps this is a metaphor for my life, falling into water and nearly drowning, and then someone coming to my rescue.

In fact sometime later, at a BBQ (barbeque) at my Uncle Bill's house in Seaford (Long Island), a drunk adult picked me up from behind, while in mid air I dropped the hot dog I held in my hand, and he tossed me into my uncle's pool! I couldn't swim, too young to learn; it felt like an eternity on the bottom, then somehow splashing up for air. Billy Collins, the poet, had it right, "As you sink toward the weedy disarray of the bottom, leaving behind what you have already forgotten, the surface, now overrun with the high travel of clouds." I'd never forget the fear, and a certain exhilaration. I'll always remember what I saw first when resurfacing: the nighttime clouds in the sky.

My sister-moms shared the room next to my brother and me, three of them crammed into the only other room on the second floor. They had a better view of the street, the trees, the grass, and the passersby. I often went there, to play with their make-up or my sister Anne's clown dolls. Once I watched our Italian neighbor Cesarino Infante chase and hit his son Jimmy with a metal pole. I found out later that Jimmy had been experimenting with cocaine and marijuana. We had one bathroom for seven people, and the doors on the second floor had no locks. Looking back I wish they did, as it might have helped us to understand and to honor boundaries. In any case, my sisters were very, very different, each unique.

Anne had the greatest influence on my childhood. I would spend the most time with her; we'd shop, and I mean shop! She'd take me to the Green Acres Mall, to stores like A&S, Alexander's, Sterns, or Kay Bee Toys, and she'd buy and buy and buy clothes. She'd buy me toys. I loved the department stores, enjoyed watching her try on clothes as if I were her personal shopper. She'd take me to class at CUNY-Hunter College; she'd also learn how to hone her skills at giving psychological exams by testing my friends and me. I was her chief admirer, and I grew surprisingly close to her.

My middle sister Elizabeth was the most independent of the three. She suffered from epilepsy, a neurological disorder that struck her with seizures, adding to the instability of my home life. Sometimes when my dad would be in a rage, my sister would seize, and my family would rush into crisis mode. At the time, Elizabeth was rail thin, gorgeous, the prettiest of the three. But she was deeply affected by her disabling illness, her freedom compromised, and so her subsequent flourishing thwarted. When I couldn't sleep at night, Elizabeth gave me a stuffed animal named Odie, the dog from the cartoon Garfield. In terms of object relation's theory, this stuffed animal became my security blanket. Later, she'd enroll in the School of Visual Arts, but her potential as a photographer suffered from her loyalty to the sputtering *American Legacy Magazine*, where she worked as a marketing director.

My youngest sister Catharine was my chief tormentor; her actions affected my youth in significantly negative ways. Whether I was publicly bubble-bathed by her and her friends, or made to watch a Nightmare on Elm Street at 6 years old, or left in our attic with no way to get out, she made it her business to terrify me. After watching Freddy Krueger slash Johnny Depp to death while eating pizza bagels with my sister and her friends, I could not go alone into my basement or boiler room. I was terrified that Freddy would enter my dreams and kill me. In the cold of the winter, the hissing radiator in my bedroom tormented me, "Freddy's after me!" and I would scream, which is when the Odie stuffed animal served as my protector. When my mom would sometimes send me to retrieve something in the basement, my sister would shut the lights off. I'd be frozen in terror until I could scream, but the lights would not be turned on. Then I'd run, petrified that Freddy or the night or the night terror would be coming after me.

As a gay, African-American author James Baldwin writes in his essay, *Many Thousands Gone*, "We cannot escape our origins, however hard we try, those origins which contain the key—could we but find it—to all that we later become." These were my roots; I keep looking at them and questioning their influence on my life. Of course, I did all this in search of self-knowledge because I'd always taken seriously the Greek exhortation, "Know thyself."

These were my formative years at the Brenkert household, subsequently entering Kindergarten at Clear Stream Avenue School. I possessed no boundaries, was impulsive and out-of-control, which won no favor from my teachers or peers. I was called "the Kissing Bandit" because I tried to kiss the girls and look up their skirts. I thought it was funny, but not the girls. One day I had an accident in the bathroom, which resulted in more alienation. I wanted to connect with my classmates, but they seemingly didn't want to connect with me. And I was soon shuttled off to a new progressive and innovative program called Special Education. All the adults around me wanted me to practice self-control. I thought, what's wrong with boys today! Aren't boys imaginative, creative, aggressive, jealous, and playful? All of this was very disconcerting to a lonely and confused little boy.

I sought comfort in the place I visited regularly, the Church of the Blessed Sacrament where I prayed and felt safe; also played by running up and down the aisles. Afterwards, sitting in a pew, I'd gaze at the beautiful corpus of Jesus hanging from the cross, his bare-chested body, his muscles, his abs, and his eyes. Something about that body struck me: it was a man's but it was beautiful. I loved Jesus very much.

At home in the privacy of my room, I'd pray to Jesus and would come to have a very different personal relationship with my faith than with my family. My family was steeped in the tradition of the Catechism of the Catholic Church and the St. Joseph Baltimore Catechism, the standard catechisms of Catholic doctrine and dogma, used in American Catholic high schools from 1885 to the 1960s. The Baltimore Catechism replaced the Jesuit Robert Bellarmine's *Small Catechism*, an earlier attempt to create a uniform and universal, though brief, explanation of the Catholic faith for use by Catholics worldwide. Such catechisms did not speak about the interior life of the person of faith, they read like axioms, bulleted points that parents could use to scold, to punctiliously "form" their impish, impudent or pugnacious children. Thankfully, I was experiencing an intimate relationship with God, one at once reciprocal, active, alive, so resonant that it filled me with gratitude.

That's how it started, my love of Jesus and my faith in him. In the locus of faith, I felt secure and safe, where I need not wear a mask, where I could simply be myself: Ben; thus, I was at peace and felt exquisitely alive. I loved dressing up for the holy days in suit, tie, and jacket. I loved the church music. I loved the good priests, who to me seemed androgynous: They could sing, but they could also articulate the inner life, and in the outer life they wore vestments, incensed the sacred space of the altar, and they taught the Gospel, about life here and hereafter. I was happiest serving as their altar boy.

I admired the priests' love of their parishioners, as well as their love and concern for the poor. They countered my parents' fears of minorities, and they taught us how as a community and as individuals to handle fear, anxiety and worry. I felt as if they were speaking directly to me, and I was riveted. At Blessed Sacrament, they taught that God's love is limitless, that He is omnipresent. They presented saints as icons of holiness, and I learned to model my life on St. Francis of Assisi and St. Anthony of Padua. In short, my life was in their hands, hands forming me for one thing only: to love God and to let God love me.

When I look back at my growing up, I see that on Fir Street, there were many families with children, and we'd play manhunt, tag, TV tag or street hockey. We'd play basketball; ride our bikes; run and play, lost in our imaginations. I could name every car that passed by just by identifying its grill, like the popular American car, the 1992 Chevrolet Caprice Classic. On this street, there was also a lot of fear, a lot of drinking. I could smell alcohol on the breath of every dad. On the streets of my neighborhood, where curfews came and went, I learned about divisions in friendships, how to make allies, how to make friends, in short, how to survive.

At this time, I observed the boys on my block. We had begun to look at each other differently. We stared unabashedly at each other longer and later did some innocent sexual things, like showing each other our penises, certainly a rite of passage that a gay boy like me enjoyed. I found myself sexually attracted to two guys, Mark Captain, the hot blonde-haired, blue-eyed jock at the other end of our block, and my favorite male camp counselor who, when he suddenly stopped working, I wept.

I knew I liked boys, for example, Joey McIntyre and the other New Kids on the Block. I'd sing *Hanging Tough* or *Please Don't Go Girl* and decorated my bedroom with posters of boys from the NKOTB. My dad told me boys don't sing, only girls. As a result, I dropped out of the school's chorus. My dad, often drunk, warred with my mom. My dad used drink as an escape from his depression, but it only sank him deeper and deeper into desolation and rancor. I felt great sorrow for him.

What had I liked about the boys on my block? Pretty much everything: their spirit, hair, eyes and lips. I wasn't attracted to all of them, Victor Anjelo was too heavy, and too feminine, Valentino Infante too fearful, too often by his mother's side. I loved it when we were shirtless, for during swimming or playing baseball or soccer, I'd have glimpses of their bodies.

In elementary school, I'd been a misfit, living on the fringe. I once told Susan Grisly, the school's most popular girl, also a member of the Church choir, that I liked the New Kids on the Block. She used this information as a weapon against me; to her only girls were allowed to like the New Kids, and she made it sting by telling everyone "our" little secret. That was fourth grade. When in sixth grade Susan Grisly started to fondle me in the library during movies, I was exasperated. The lights would go off, the movie would turn on and within seconds her hand went down my pants. And even when she brought my hand down to touch her vagina, I just froze. I dissociated. I disappeared. Who would've believed that this popular girl was interested in me?

But in sixth grade, I also shared a class with Samuel Beckett, the boy who took every unkind insult (gay, queer, fag) from everyone, including me. I don't know if Samuel and I knew that we were attracted to each other in sixth grade, but by the eighth grade we were always together.

There were other guys I liked (Samuel was a faithful stand-by). I remember James, a peer in my summer school program in Oceanography. He turned me on! But I was afraid to approach him. I can remember looking through the phone books, and finding the number for another boy I liked, Rick Steele, a cute preppy, lacrosse player, who spoke with a lisp. I'd call his house and listen for him to answer, and when he did, I would hang up. (If the Church were more affirming of the teenage-me as a gay person perhaps I'd have been more bold, *e.g.*, asking Rick on a date. But at that time, the Church did not form the gay person, instead She preferred homophobia or to see the need to save the whole person. But being gay was never part of who I am: it has been always Who God made me to be. I believe it is homophobic to suggest a gay person has a gay part (sic tendency) of his being, it suggests that one's gayness is not part of their humanity, and the consequences of such rhetoric include stigma, discrimination and antipathy for gay men.)

At this time, I had set up an Internet Avatar through AOL. My screen name was BJ69NY. I'd enter chat rooms, start and end abrupt virtual conversations. (That virtual and remote world was far different from the highly developed virtual and remote world running about on high speed internet during the COVID 19 pandemic.) It was nothing that I really wanted, but I pursued it because in such anonymity I could be myself. And I was connected to people like me. And to be candid, there were plenty of men attracted to BJ69NY, though I never arranged to meet them. The one I did end up writing became obsessed with me, incessantly telephoning my home, sending me semi-nudes in the mail. His name was something akin to the sinister Roger Chillingworth of Nathaniel Hawthorne's *The Scarlet Letter*. My mom had no idea what was going on with me, and this boy from Connecticut. Every time he called a chill went down my spine. I was so relieved when he stopped calling.

During this time, I started to hear another kind of calling, one much more loving thus more welcomed, this one from God: a calling to me to become a Catholic priest. My parish's associate pastor Fr. Abraham Pardoen, a diocesan priest on loan from Sri Lanka, had asked me if I ever seriously considered the priesthood. He must have observed in me something about which I was totally unaware. What did a fifteen year old, with BJ69NY for an AOL screen name, with an alcoholic dad, with a mom who rejected her gay son, a gay kid with anorexia, who stalked boys, a person who found peace in God's Church, really know?

From that moment on, I discerned my vocation to the priesthood with the Diocese of Long Island. What attracted me was not only God's invitation to me, (for was not Fr. Abraham God's intermediary, as I had been taught?), but also the potential, as a gay priest, to make a difference in the life of LGBTQ youth, they who shared my story, boys and girls who may have felt unloved if not rejected by their family, and who hadn't heard that God loves them unconditionally, that God from the very beginning always loves them and accepts them.

As a gay priest, I could enter a ministry that would reach out to these young people struggling to accept and to be themselves. Because of my life experience I was at a great advantage because I fully understood that they had no one to affirm them, to accept them, to love them. They were not allowed to be themselves, not accepted by a Church decades away from having a Pope like Pope Francis I, a Church that insists that people with same-sex attraction are objectively disordered, while their same-sex acts are intrinsically evil. I do not believe that Jesus condemns gays nor does he condemn the expression of gay love. I took my prayer, prevenient grace, and my conviction that God loves me to discernment, and to the vocation program in the Diocese of Rockville Centre.

I remember one candidate who showed up for a weekend Fr. Tim Howard conducted at the Seminary of the Immaculate Conception. I'll call him Charlie, because I forget his name. He showed up in a green Cadillac, and from the moment I saw him, I was strongly attracted to him. But his time in my life was brief (76 hours!). I came away from that weekend meeting feeling I could not be a diocesan priest because of my sexuality. There was also another reason: The men I met at the seminary were cold, repressed and fragmented. Thus, I decided that for me, at 18, to choose celibacy wasn't prudent. At the time, I had to accept the reality that I possessed too strong a libido.

So I entered Marist College, where I continued to discern my vocation, while also settling into my human skin. I immediately got a job with Fr. Lyle McPherson as the Chaplain's Assistant; he interviewed me in his bathrobe over mint chocolate chip ice cream. Within the first few weeks of school I had a good paying job, and I started drinking. Why did I drink? I was homesick; I was also a closeted teenager at a rigidly conservative school, one that my mom had chosen, not me. I was confused. No one at home had ever modeled how to drink or how to share emotions or things that mattered personally. Of course, I never spoke candidly or freely about my sexuality at home; this remains mostly the case today.

I started drinking recklessly. My time on the crew team was brief, but I met my closest buddy, Marlon Aquila, there; he helped me through homesickness, and he taught me how to drink gin. Drinking quickly became a problem for me, but I wouldn't join a program of recovery, where I'd discuss my experience, strength and hope until 2012. Usually I would pregame at the Sheehan Hall, our dormitory, and then head out to one of the off-campus frat houses. Not only would I get drunk, but I'd often pass out, or be put to sleep. Once when I was blackout drunk, I went back to my RA's (resident assistant) room, and we started getting undressed; he was gay, some years older. I didn't like the feeling of his hairy legs, or hairy crotch, and so I begged him to stop; when he wouldn't, I said I'm going to be sick, and he finally released me run to his bathroom. Where not long after EMTs (emergency medical technician) were assessing my condition, after they threw my head against the toilet I vomited, and was taken by ambulance to St. Francis Hospital. I was humiliated as they carried me out of the dorm on a gurney. They called my mom. No one in my family, however, knew that I (at eighteen) was feeling unequivocally starved and desperate for human touch.

While at Marist, I imagined myself becoming a priest in a religious order, perhaps a Marist brother. But on second thought, I never felt called to be a brother but to be a priest. Brother James Nice helped me discover my vocation; he was a clinical psychologist. I was assigned to him because of my drinking. He and I met weekly. When he came out to me, I knew that I could come out to him, and I did. The next turning point for me came on September 11, 2001.

The world had changed, and America was on alert. I discerned that life had to be lived, that any unnecessary falsifying of my identity had to be stopped. I took on a "fuck-the-world" mindset because evil had fucked the world anyway. I waited until Thanksgiving to come out for the second time. (The first time I tried to come out I was 14, my sister, Catharine, and my mom told me I'd burn in hell. I opted for the closet; my coming out a failure. I felt completely rejected). This time my mom stopped speaking to me for three months. It's a terrible thing to be motherless. Why wouldn't this Catholic mom accept and love me? She knew I was discerning a call to the priesthood, that my relationship with Jesus was serious and intimate, so why could she not understand? What did I have to do to earn her acceptance and love? If God accepts me, why doesn't she?

Those three months passed slowly, but my mom and I eventually spoke. In a sense, our relationship started over. But as with my siblings and my dad, my mom didn't want me to speak about my attraction to men or about the men I'd dated. She dismissed it all as phase, saying that she'd pray to God that I'd change. I wanted to say, "Mom, I'm gay and I'll always be gay no matter how much you pray. Why not just accept the fact that this is the way God made me?" But saying that would be futile. (Some years later mom and me, then a Jesuit Seminarian would travel to Spain and Italy, pilgrims on the road like St. Ignatius. I joyed in taking her abroad for the first and only time in her lovely life.)

I ruled out entering the Marist Fathers my senior year of college, even though I'd been accepted into their Novitiate. I decided that I wasn't really attracted to this small conservative order located in Boston. It was about this time that I learned about my acceptance to schools of social work and met the Society of Jesus (the Jesuits) for the first time. As I committed to CUNY-Hunter College for graduate school, I requested more and more information from the Jesuits.

In my junior and senior year classes at Marist College, I met Matteo Ricci, Walter Ciszek and the Jesuits of the Reductions in Latin America. These were deeply talented men, religious men who were both worldly and unworldly; they were companions of Jesus and friends of the poor. I identified with them, their apostolic spirit, and their ability to find God in all things. My interest in the Jesuits led to my reading poems by Gerard Manley Hopkins as well as my printing everything I could from the New York Province of the Society of Jesus homepage. The Internet birthed my vocation to the Jesuits; I am ever thankful to www.nysj.org.

I was most struck by the story of Fr. Walter Ciszek, the Jesuit who spent 23 years in the Soviet Union, most of which he spent as a slave in the labor camps in Siberia. In his deeply moving personal story *He Leadeth Me* Walter Ciszek questioned God's presence while the Red Army pillaged towns and villages, causing inestimable misery among people. Ciszek often pondered the question: "Why has God allowed this evil to happen?" And I thought about his question as it related to my own perplexity and pain as a gay Catholic, "Why has God made me gay, yet called me always her Child?" But even in my own suffering, I understood, like Ciszek, that one could "be faithful to God and to look to him in everything, confident of his love and his constancy, aware that this world and this new order was not our lasting city any more than the previous one had been, and striving always to know his will and to do it each day of our lives."

Ciszek's understanding of the priesthood nourished my own desire to be priestly. Ciszek writes that a priest, "In his role as another Christ, as a mediator between God and men . . . could offer up his suffering and his labors for his fellowmen." I too wanted to offer up, to serve, to be generous, to put others needs before my own, to see what God sees in humanity. This is why Ciszek became my Jesuit-patron saint, and why one day, I'm certain, he will be canonized by a future Pope.

There is something about the Jesuits, their talents, ambitions, radical hospitality and commitment to social justice that made me feel that I myself was lacking—something. I admit this even though I was awarded a job with Senator Hillary Rodham Clinton in the summer 2002. My feelings of inadequacy led me to suspend discernment, resulting in my ripping up everything I printed concerning the Jesuit way of proceeding. I hadn't realized at that moment that I was very much a kindred spirit of Saint Ignatius of Loyola, that Basque nobleman and founder of the Society of Jesus.

By the spring of 2003, I was a mess and hit rock bottom. I left graduate school and landed a job at Ruby Tuesday's serving beers and burgers to Long Island's best. I had also had a restraining order against my ex-boyfriend, who had threatened my life and said that he had infected me with AIDS. Thankfully he stayed away. I prayed to the Virgin Mary and begged her to ask her son Jesus to help me. About this time I started wearing my miraculous medal, which only comes off during surgery. Because she answered my prayers, I returned to Mary often, and then more easily turned to her son.

I spent several months in private discernment. I didn't want to eat 5-course meals with Bishops or take side trips to Novitiates unless it was real, unless God verified my calling in my private prayer. I still felt a call to help those LGBTQ youth fractured and fragmented by both society and religion. I also felt called to the sacraments, to celebrating Mass, to Christ in the Eucharist and to Reconciliation.

I wrote an email to Fr. Paul Arnold, S.J., who worked at the Jesuit-run retreat house on Long Island. I confessed to him that I was openly gay, that I had been discerning a calling since I was fifteen, that I wanted to meet him to enter a discernment process about entering the Society of Jesus. In my email, I reinforced the fact that I was not running away from my sexuality, that I would not be forced back into the closet, that the Society of Jesus would have to accept me as I am.

Paul responded kindly, as any son of Saint Ignatius of Loyola or Jesuit might. He simply said, sure let's meet. I was encouraged by his response, so much so I that went to observe what the kind of spirituality/life the Jesuits offered. And I learned quickly: It is about generosity, loyalty, hospitality and the stewardship of the poor and children. I learned that most Jesuits were deeply affective human beings; I was also surprised to learn that many Jesuits are gay. I always questioned Fr. Paul's sexuality. We often spoke about our being religious and about what a gay man like me might experience in our Post 9/11 world. He gave me the works of the Catholic theologian Fr. James Alison, beyond Alison the literature on gays and Roman Catholicism was dint. Once, Fr. Paul and I talked about "gaydar," that interior voice that tells the gay man that the person he is speaking with is gay, or that couple sitting across from you at dinner are gay. I lamented that some people have better gaydar, chiding heterosexual people who could tell someone was gay more easily than us.

Fr. Paul told me about his heroes, gay-friendly Jesuits like Frs. Rory Sanz, or his classmate, Rick Dandelion, men who helped him through his own second-class citizenship as a less popular Jesuit. Was I wet behind the ears? Perhaps, but I did listen to and hear Fr. Paul's message: some gay priests, in the Society of Jesus, as in the outside world, were psychologically healthier than others. We spoke about the reasons behind some gay men choosing the veil of the priesthood, to run away from their sexuality or sex, still others who entered the priesthood for the *right* reasons, because Jesus loves them, just the same as straight men, they, like me were absolutely convinced of this. Fr. Paul and I even lamented Pope Emeritus Benedict XVI's stern recommendation that no gay man be allowed to enter the seminary or religious life unless he was celibate for a period of time.

And as I met more and more Jesuits, including Fr. Jerry Mettlesome, I grew confident that in this order I, as a gay Catholic, could pursue God's will for me. I felt rekindled by what I call the pre-Corporate Society of Jesus, a Society of Jesus much closer to her roots than that of the Society today, a Society of Jesus much more in touch with humanity, one that lived closer to the poor, one that more easily confronted the Catholic hierarchy, a Society of Jesus before I-phones and Facebook and The Jesuit Post. This was the Society of Jesus that I entered at age 25, in August 2005.

Chapter 2

Al's Silver Bullet

MY DAD, ALBERT, ALWAYS sweat profusely. He dripped with sweat in the sweltering summer, after a bath in the winter, after smoking a cigarette in the spring, even after drinking a 6-pack of Schmidt's beer in the fall; even in his deathbed photo, in 2010, he looked at me wet with sweat. I remember sawing a piece of wood with him one summer afternoon. We needed wood anchors to support the air conditioners in our rooms so each summer we'd install the air conditioners in the bedrooms, but my dad never kept the wood anchors alongside the stored air conditioners. He'd worry so much about the windows, obsessively afraid that the air conditioners might fall from the window frame, perhaps hurting or killing someone.

He also hated spending his money on the electric bill, his body baking and sweating in the living room while watching summer reruns of the television series *Matlock* or *In the Heat of the Night*. Although my mom, Loretta insisted that we have an air conditioner in the living room, it didn't arrive until the late 1990s.

I'd watch dad while he was cutting a two-by-four; he breathed harder, faster, sweat spurting from his forehead and from under his arms. By no means was he fit. His usual attire was his favorite Dockers (khakis), a white t-shirt that covered his belly and the same pair of white tennis shoes. Even at 10 years old, I'd watch my dad, making "my" mental notes. In general, he was like most American fathers, worked hard but didn't take care of himself.

Dad hardly spoke, but I sensed he had a lot to say. His mute rage commanded attention. Although I feared him, I also loved him tremendously. I loved him like any son loves a dad, not merely because he was my dad, but because I was from his loins, had his genes.

I also loved him because I believed that he was much more than his manic depression or his alcoholism. I loved him because of his age, rendering him vulnerable, more susceptible to injury. I worried about his health. I feared God might take him at any moment. But there was that other ominous side of him, the mercurial temperament, one moving from silence to rage in an instant. This gave me the impression of strength and power, but I knew deep inside that my real dad was essentially a sweet, sensitive, loving, funny man. I can't reduce my dad to T.S. Eliot's "formulaic phrase" because he was essentially a mystery, one that kept him distant from me, nearly locking me out. But I'll always treasure my memories of him, and these keep me close to him, even now after his death.

Dad made the best damn French toast from New York City to Montauk. It was a rare holiday occasion when my dad made his French toast, and he certainly made it count, using a cast-iron skillet and making just enough slices of bread to make our Tudor-home smell like maple syrup. On Christmas mornings I remember waking up, opening the presents, devouring his French toast and going to Mass, a tradition our family treasured.

Some nine years after dad's death, I still snooped through his dresser drawers for clues to his identity, handling items (*sic* relics) as mundane as dice, tie clips, a pin of the Virgin Mary, army dog tags, an onyx ring, elastic band watches, prayer cards. (I did this until my parent's home was sold in March 2020.) I'd fiddle with them, hear them clank as I drop them back into the drawer. I wish my dad had told me why he kept them. And because I don't know the facts (except that my dad was a good, abundantly loving man), I can only speculate: Was he racked with guilt, guilt that rose from his core because his mom died after complications of labor during childbirth of his youngest brother, and intensified at the death of his youngest brother months later? Such trauma is revelation; it says, or at least implies, much of my dad's character. I'll never know if my dad's depression, loneliness, and solitude, or his loving, generous and humorous spirit collided that day, only to pursue and torture him during a lifetime of desolation and consolation.

Dad finished high school and served in Germany during the Korean War. He was eight years older than my mom, growing up on the same street as she in Maspeth, Queens. He went from civil service job to civil service job, working stints with the New York City Sanitation Department, Police Department and finally the Fire Department. He had two other brothers Raymond and William.

When we'd visit my uncles' homes, my dad would drink with them. He loved his brothers, and they got along, and he wasn't silent with them.

Usually we went to my Uncle Ray's house for the Fourth of July, where his three sons and one daughter would host us along with my larger-than-life Irish aunt, Eileen. I loved the playful but drunken banter between Uncle Ray and Aunt Eileen. They were a real life version of Ralph and Alice Cramden from television's *Honeymooners*, but unlike Ralph, my uncle was an alcoholic. I loved the way my aunt would put him in his place, fearless in contradicting him. My dad loved it too. I can't say what my mom thought.

When the sun set, my cousins, who were older than I, would display the grandest fireworks show outside New York City. Two of them were cops, one a firefighter, and they knew every Nassau County cop that drove down the block in East Meadow. There were more booze and fireworks than I care to remember. It's amazing no one got hurt. When it came time for my dad to drive us home, he was usually drunk. He'd argue with my mom about his driving home, and my mom would relent. I'd be scooped up, placed in the car and away we went. Thankfully I had "carcolepsy" and would fall asleep as soon as the car hit the highway. I'd wake up, and we'd be home. Then "Al's Silver Bullet" arrived.

In 1991 my dad bought a silver Honda Accord. It was the first time he'd departed from buying General Motors. He gave our last Ford Motor Company's Zephyr to my sister Anne, but it soon met its end in a rainstorm, and our Pontiac Grand Prix went to my youngest sister Catharine. My middle sister Liz was banned from driving because she had epilepsy. My mom, who was the only parent working at the time, shared the new car with my dad. The new Honda Accord was quickly termed Al's Silver Bullet, but to me it was more ironic, for the car's nickname had nothing to do with how fast my dad drove, after all he drove very slowly. I surmised that the nickname of the car had more to do with the name of my dad's new favorite beer, Coors Light. At the time Coors was starting their ad campaign that nicknamed their Rocky Mountain brew "the silver bullet." The ice-cold Rocky Mountain beer made for many drunken nights, and with each drunken night my dad slipped even slower into the dark night of the soul, the place where depression and one's darkest thoughts fester and grow and germinate more and more lies, lies that tell truths only manic depressives believe.

As I grew up, my life at home and in school continued to be erratic and unsettled. My dad drank and my parents fought, and viciously so when my dad was drunk. My siblings could process their arguments, or at least escape the house because they were older. Much younger, I could not, having to remain inside, and I heard every hurtful word, every swear, and every vulgarity. My mom was pushed to the limits. She loved my dad and tried to meet his needs, but they were too many. Mom worked hard and managed the bills. She would want to go out on the weekend, but my dad had no interest in leaving the house, ever. But my mom believed getting him out would help. She also needed to be sociable, to be among people, to let someone else cook a meal and serve it so she could relax, a respite from cleaning, laundering, shopping, and always caring for my dad. To me, she was a saint.

Dad would hide in the basement. He'd sit in the basement and drink beer, and while everyone else engaged the world, he would retreat into further solitude, loneliness and despair. Again, I must admit, I have never understood what caused his terrible dark night; it's a mystery before which I am helpless even now as an adult.

School became a place where I could let loose the negative energy that piled up from home. I was hyper, attention seeking and impulsive. I remained very unpopular, often had the "koodies," the dreaded lurgi, all because I kissed the girls in kindergarten, looked up their skirts, and never escaped that epithet of the "kissing bandit." But I couldn't help it; I needed affection because my dad was lost on some remote inner island, and my mom worked, thus had little time for me. Yes, they provided me with love, that I do not deny, but they had each other to parent and to love, and for my mom, her top priority was caring for my dad, to preventing him from sinking deeper into the sadness and torment of his depression and alcoholism. Thus, love for me was meted out, and I naturally wanted more.

Two hospitalizations in Creedmoor Psychiatric Hospital proved that my dad's mental health issues were treatable; it takes lots of hope and trust to believe that the man you love will endure his dark night of the soul. The FDNY also cared for my dad and my mom, however, the fraternal order of fireman could only tell my mom that my dad was "sad." Psychology has come a long way in treating depression and its concomitant and co-morbid symptoms. My dad's therapy consisted of medication management sessions with a psychiatrist, but never talk therapy. Such a "no no" or worst practice in the therapeutic world. Endurance proves our finitude, our vulnerability, our need to belong (loyally) to something more than ourselves. This I learned from my mom and dad; despite their flaws and imperfections, they had to bear witness to God and redeem the horrors of the monsters within, so that evil would never be the final word. By being Good Samaritans to each other, they were never passersby, in it together, for life.

During grammar school, two big events occurred in my young life: my sister Elizabeth was diagnosed with epilepsy, and my brother William moved out of the house. Elizabeth could be Liz, Beth or Bethe. William was Bill. When my sister fell into seizure, my family instantly reacted, my dad and brother lifting and carrying her to my parent's bedroom. I was frightened because I didn't understand what was happening. Again, Mom surmised that my sister got epilepsy because she had put her tongue on an electric socket when she was a child, but my mom always had theories, but had no backup. My mom was an intelligent woman, but with five kids and an often-ailing husband, she didn't have the opportunity to seek higher education. And if she had, I know for certain that she would've pursued the cause of her child's epilepsy.

Yes, my mom was strong. She kept our family together. As I grew up, I often wondered if my mom was happy. How could she be while constantly anxious about the future? She'd expend her energy by vacuuming, ironing, washing or cooking. Upon my mom's death in 2019, I was stunned by her frugality, mesmerized by how much she denied herself materially to save money for her children. Love! Thankfully I didn't inherit worry about the future: I just did things—in the moment.

My parents were deeply religious, dare I say spiritual. They were Baltimore Catechism Roman Catholics. They were pious and insisted that their children go to the Church of the Blessed Sacrament every Sunday, and every holy day of obligation. My mom daily prayed the rosary, and my dad faithfully attended first Friday liturgy. My mom and dad had always started their day with prayers. My mom often told me that if I had been born a girl, she'd have named me Dymphna, after the saint who interceded on behalf of those suffering with nervous and emotional afflictions. Had mom projected the reality of her world onto me?

As the years went on, and the arguing increased, I often found myself in the office of Dr. Lyle Board, the school psychologist at Clear Stream Elementary School. I remember his being a kind man who let me play and talk. I had no insight into why I went there, and it only added to my missing class. By fifth grade, I was playing the clarinet and saxophone, and receiving academic support in the resource center with Ms. Jane Innocent. I must have mentioned something once to Mr. Board because my mom said that the school had called her, and implied that I was troubled by my life at home. My parents, however, were never physically abusive to me or to my siblings. Dad had never put a hand on us or on our mom. She and my dad always slept in the same bed, even on nights when the arguing was the most heated and loudest, nights when I prayed to God that my dad would stop drinking; I even prayed that my mom would separate from my dad, a sincere prayer that dissipated with the morning sun.

Some nights I'd pause my Nintendo game and get involved. I'd team up with my mom, and we'd volley his every angry word. He couldn't verbally overtake us because he was drunk. My mom tried everything from hiding the alcohol, watering down his drinks, to pouring beer down the sink. But my dad still headed out to the beer distributor, often with me in tow, and bought cases of beer with refunded beer cans.

Angry, confused and fearful, I'd smash the beer cans in our driveway. My dad didn't hear me because he was alone in the basement, staring at the TV. As an adult, I now understand that he likely felt ashamed and humiliated and chose the basement as his "refuge," a place dark and dank, with white drop ceilings, mirroring his mind and soul. I have great compassion for my dad, but as a child, I often wanted him to disappear and leave us all in peace.

At this juncture of my memoir, I am realizing the depth and breadth of my ambivalences about my dad. But I am glad that I'm recognizing them, and even as I write, I feel as if I'm understanding and integrating them.

The turning point arrived after my parents, my sister Catharine and I visited California in 1990. That year my maternal grandmother Katharine passed away. She was a Polish immigrant, and the only grandparent I knew. She lived above my Uncle Bill and his wife Mary in the same two-family home my mom grew up in, in Maspeth, Queens. Uncle Bill was the Harley Davidson driving uncle whose sons had mustaches and mullets. When my grandmother died, something happened during the reading of the will, something between my mom, her other brother Joe and Bill, that caused a rift. I wouldn't see my Uncle Bill and his family for many, many years. My mom also received some inheritance, and with it, we went to California.

My sister Catharine kept a journal, and from the moment we landed in San Francisco to the moment we left from Los Angeles, we experienced one adventure after another. We visited California in a world before emails, cell phones, beepers, or GPS devices. We did not have digital cameras, Snapchat, Facebook or Instagram. There was no TikTok dancing. We did have Catharine and her journal. She wrote about my dad's getting left on a bus in San Francisco only to turn up at the Botanical Gardens thirty minutes ahead of us. She wrote about the homeless man who tried to slip into our hotel room, about the night an air conditioner exploded in our room! She wrote about getting crapped on by sea gulls during a ferry tour of the San Francisco Bay, about nearly driving us over the cliff in the parking lot adjacent to Hearst Castle, about the time my mom had a panic attack on a bus coming home from Tijuana, Mexico. My mom had screamed when the bus came to a halt: she was claustrophobic, and there was no A/C. During that trip, my parents didn't argue; in fact, it seemed to me that they might never argue again. Was getting away, a change of scenery, just what we needed or, to be hoped for, a cure?

When we got back to Long Island, we unpacked and distributed our souvenirs. Elizabeth got a spoon; at that point she was collecting unusual or antique spoons; Anne received a doll, since she collected clown dolls; and my brother and his wife were treated to shirts and shot glasses. Married, they lived together in an apartment near Long Beach.

Over the next few years, I felt that my dad was moving into a better place (true for a short time). I couldn't tell why, but the arguing had diminished, and my parent's relationship improved. They bought a vacation house in Pennsylvania; my brother had his first daughter, Melissa. I graduated elementary school; it was 1992 and in general life was good.

I was full of gratitude and thanked God in my prayers. In those early years, I learned a lot about how serious my parents took their wedding vows and their commitment to each other to work through the good times and the bad times. I'm certain another couple might have headed for separation or divorce, but my parents held on to their marriage, not only because they were Catholic and divorce was forbidden but because they truly loved each other. My mom also believed it was God's will for her to remain with my dad, and through her love and steadfastness, he became a far better man.

That same year Al's Silver Bullet turned one. The new car smell had dissipated, but the electric seatbelts still worked like a charm, and my dad always kept the car at a cool 55 miles per hour.

Slowly but surely the beer cans returned, and Al's silver bullet became the ice cold Rocky Mountain beverage named Coors Light. With the beer again came my dad's silence and solitude, and then returned the arguing. This time I was older, and I had more independence. I was in junior high school, and my life was about to change big time: Samuel Beckett became my best friend.

As James Baldwin notes in his text *The Fire Next Time*, "God gave Noah the rainbow sign, no more water but fire next time." I was about to enter not water but the fire of teenage sex.

Chapter 3

LongIslandm4m18to24

SOMETIME IN 1994 AMERICA on Line (AOL) started mailing CDs to homes across the United States. Each CD contained free software that led users to the Internet. My mom and dad had no idea what the Internet was, and was, to them a radical, new "thing" much like interracial marriage or African-Americans moving into the suburbs. For this young gay-teenager in the early 1990s, AOL was like a gateway drug, except the high came not from substance use but from interacting with men across Long Island. I didn't know about the history of Stonewall or the Gay Rights Movement, and the comedian Ellen DeGeneres was still three years from coming out publicly as a lesbian, but some years earlier my parents did take me to a "gay" restaurant in Portland, Maine. We were on our way to Nova Scotia and stopped off in a pub that seated mostly men. It's all I can remember about the setting, except for my mom's quips about the looks we got, which seemed to ask, "Who are these breeders and their son?"

The virtual world of gay men, gay sex seemed a far safer reality than the hostile reality I lived in. By fourteen, I understood all-too-well that the Roman Catholic Church teaches that homosexuality and homosexual acts are "acts of grave depravity," that "tradition has always declared that homosexual acts are intrinsically disordered" and that "this inclination, which is objectively disordered, constitutes for most of them a trial," which meant I would be a "safe" outsider or fringe character in two worlds, two worlds that rejected me for the person God created.

My home's perspective: I'd burn in hell for being gay; Church teaching: I was intrinsically disordered; and my natural inclinations and attractions towards men were contrary to natural law and culture. *What a prison, what a cup of trembling!* As the metaphysical poet, John Donne said, "batter my heart three person'd God." It was because of the loss of connection to my family and my Church that I had never developed stable gay friendships. Instead, and when not in religious life, I'd be relegated to isolation because my family and my Church formed me to distrust myself and homosexuals, hence even today, my circle of non-gay Jesuit friends is small, and I continue to rebuild old friendships and find new friends who are gay.

Looking back on my family and my Church, I can see that both worlds lacked insight, insight in the manner which the twentieth century theologian Bernard Lonergan spoke about opening oneself up to the human, to the dynamic of the human spirit, a movement well beyond understanding, experience and judgment. Insight allows people to discern their humanity, to be able to empathize, to suffer in the face of suffering. St. Ignatius of Loyola understood this fact, that his *Spiritual Exercises* provides exercises in prayer, meditation and contemplation that offer a person insight into one's relationship with God, self and other. The *Spiritual Exercises* are Ignatius' gift to the Church and to the world; through it, prayers learn how to spiritually flourish as part of the group called humanity, humanity that is and always will be part of creation.

I hadn't known that my family and my Church's love for me, unlike God's, was conditional. Nor had I realized that the Roman Catholic Church had equated her teaching in the Catechism of the Catholic Church (CCC 2351–2359) on homosexuality with fornication, rape, masturbation and prostitution as offenses to the vocation of chastity, so serious a sin that it demanded damnation.

I suffered from anxiety, internalized homophobia, preventing me from integrating my inner world and my outer world. AOL and the Internet helped alleviate my need to reconcile these worlds, while my religion (Lat. *re-ligere*, to connect) and growing spirituality helped keep God and Jesus close to me. I asked myself over and over, how could I be Catholic and gay? I was loved by my Church and my family, but did they really love me? Thankfully, I trusted enough in God's mercy and providential love; otherwise, I'd just be following a tradition that begins with a talking snake. First, I needed to journey into my soul, to process my sexual identity through adolescence, to integrate my faith and sexuality. Second, I could no longer hide from myself or my human needs; I needed human touch because one cannot live without it.

Before my sister Elizabeth brought home a refurbished laptop, which did nothing more than connect me to the Internet via dial-up, I went online at my friend Samuel Beckett's house. Samuel's first screen name was

JustCasualSB79; mine was BJ69NY. Our screen names revealed, publicly, our desires and motivations. Samuel's screen name suggested he was looking for "sexual fun" and mine stood for blowjob, the sexual position 69 and my location, New York.

When my friends Donatella Ojeda, whose screen name was GirlyD186, and Sharon Libowitz, whose screen name was babyblueyedfriend confronted me about the meaning of my screen name, I blushed and explained: Benjamin James, my marching-band folder-number (69)! and the state I live in, New York. What young teen or man out for sex would not message JustCasualSB79 or BJ69NY? AOL changed our world forever; playing a seminal part in both my coming-of-age and my coming-out story. Mostly though, when I reflect on my adolescence, I realize that without Samuel Beckett that I might not have made it through puberty.

I met Samuel at Clear Stream Avenue Elementary School. We weren't friends, but I'd always known about him. He was the token feminine boy, the prototypical school "fag," "homo" and "queer"—as he was called by our peers. Samuel had feminine features, was slim with manicured hands, had deep raisin brown eyes, and his mom dressed him to look scrubbed clean and preppy, surely a mommy's boy.

As the kissing bandit, I didn't need any other negative attention. Girls like Carmela Montefiore, Rosa Valentina, Melissa Holiday, Jessica Innocent, Susan Grisly and Darla Sedgwick had already bullied me daily. I never knew why or how Samuel became friends with these girls, but he also hung out with Karen Coolidge, our gym teacher, Ms. C.'s favorite pet. Ms. C. was a hefty woman, likely a former basketball player, and she loved Karen. I remember when Ms. C. and our other teachers dressed up in raisin suits and sang songs by the California Raisins, a hilarious memory that I can't seem to forget.

Samuel also attended after school catechism, called CCD, at the Church of the Blessed Sacrament. We'd be in class but hardly talked. Soon we were making our First Holy Communion. Dressed in my navy suit, I realized I felt safer and happier in Church. I had been bullied relentlessly in elementary school, but at CCD the situation was different; maybe my peers were tired, or they understood that being Christian meant being nice, well, at least for the hour of class. Perhaps they felt guilty when they heard the parable of the Good Samaritan, at least I wanted them to feel remorse for their ill treatment of me.

I loved religion class, studying the beatitudes, memorizing the commandments, being taught how to serve the poor. My affection for religion became infectious, and unlike my siblings who gossiped during mass, I developed a prayer life at a very young age. It was God and me, Jesus and me, the Saints and me; I'd turn to them when my parents' arguments went violent; I turned to them when I was unhappy.

By age twelve I prayed nightly, mostly intercessory prayers from my bed, praying for God to make things better at home, to let the violence end, to stop the bullying at school, and to help me make more friends. It was too true that the girls who bullied me affected my relationships with male peers like Pablo Valentino, Mark Captain and Jorge Dominguez. I could never enter their inner circle. I had "friended" Leonicio Corona, my friend from diapers, and Matthew Gallagher, my friend from Special Education at Shaw Avenue Elementary School. Our love for activities like the World Wrestling Federation (WWF) and Nintendo bonded us. Leonicio and Matthew and I were huge fans of Sigourney Weaver and the Aliens series. When I slept over at their house, we'd watch Aliens, maybe A Nightmare on Elm Street (because I still had nightmares about Freddy!) or play video games until the early morning.

Out of school I played street hockey with the boys on my block, but in school, I was like an untouchable member of the Indian caste system. I always felt like an alien; hence I grew shyer, and overweight. I noticed that I was happiest when thinking about God, going to Church with my family, observing the priests celebrate mass. I was fond of younger priests like Fr. Tim and Fr. Joe, young enthusiastic pastors, men who spoke well, but who also didn't discriminate. Fr. Tim and Fr. Joe were priests for everyone, my early heroes, and no one held claim to them, as everyone received their affection equally. To me they had no favorites; by them I was liked as much as the popular kids. Such kind behavior was what drew me to Jesus: his radical welcome, his generosity, his ability to comfort me when I needed someone to love, and who loves me. To me the priest stood *in persona Christi*, an imitator of Jesus Christ, and the priest's embrace was psychological, even mystical, but never physical. All of this was part and parcel of an incipient spirituality, and God became more and more important to me.

About the same time Samuel and I had our first class together, with Mr. Cartwright. It was sixth grade. Everyone knew about the "Cartwright Clutch" and everyone knew to avoid it. We'd heard about it since Kindergarten, and we'd seen it in action. Mr. Cartwright would take his powerful hand and squeeze the back of a boy's neck; he'd squeeze it and bring the kid closer to his body and look them straight in the eyes: they knew they did something bad, and Mr. Cartwright made sure they felt it. I never experienced the "Cartwright Clutch," but my peer, Sean D'Agastino had, and it made him cry. As such, Cartwright was the only teacher known for still becoming abusively physical with his students. He was the only other male teacher, second to Mr. Lawrence, who had done nothing but assist in my alienation in Kindergarten.

Mr. Lawrence along with Mrs. Monday had sent me off to special education as an outcast, to a land of rejects. I've always wondered, "What were you thinking?" or "Why didn't you do anything to stop my peers from bullying me?" For instance, after I had an accident in the bathroom, where I had diarrhea, and had made a mess of myself, I asked the girl in the next stall to "go, get Mr. Lawrence." He came into the stall, saw me, and helped me out, but Amy Olmert heard everything. She subsequently left the bathroom and informed all our peers that I shit myself. From that moment on, not one kid would share even a crayon with me without my crying first.

By sixth grade, I already had a crush on boys from my elementary school, a crush on teenage boy characters from the cartoon *The Bionic Six* and a crush on a camp counselor who had suddenly stopped working at summer camp during 1988 or 1989. I liked my camp counselor's boyish looks, his effeminate, young features, his eyes, and his voice. With money I saved I'd buy videotapes (VHS) and play the New Kids in the Block in concert. I'd do this alone, because I had no idea what my friends or my family might think. I identified with *The Bionic Six's* superhero son Eric Bennett who was ruggedly athletic. When the series was canceled in 1989, I was devastated.

I can't remember my camp counselor's name, but I do remember how sensitive he was, and that he had a swimmer's build. He had blonde hair, and I often looked for him after changing from my swimming trunks. Then one day he was gone, no one knew anything, but I knew that I missed him because I was attracted to him, maybe infatuated. I asked the counselor who drove me home from camp a series of questions about his disappearance. And the fact that I so vividly remember him says a lot about me as a gay boy.

By 1992, at twelve years old, I definitely knew I was attracted to boys. Unlike other boys, I enjoyed shopping with my sister Anne, who'd take me to the Green Acres mall after school to shop. I was her buyer, reviewer and admirer. While Anne racked up credit card debt, I met her friends, young women like Rosa Hillebrand who smelled like flowers, and who had lovely hair. I liked watching them apply make-up, and I liked telling my sister how beautiful she looked in the latest fashions. Anne also let me shift her standard cars into gear when she drove. It was so much fun; her grey Nissan Sentra looked like a silver box. It had an electrical number code that was required to start the car, high tech security for the late 1980s. We went everywhere together, until I opted to play with the boys on my block.

Fir Street was also home to the Astorinos, Infantes, Batales, Anjelos, Wooleys and Captains. Before long my neighbors included Romanians,

Indians and Latinos. One of the Anjelos was hot for my Romanian neighbor's niece. She was a tennis prodigy who had been sent to America to work on her serve and volley. She was very attractive, had long black hair, fine facial features, a strong abdomen, and was also multi-lingual. Sometimes she'd come out of her house to play, but her uncle, Mitch, would sweep her up, bringing her inside lest we Americans "Americanize" her.

By this time I learned how to survive, how to be resilient, how to adjust to my surroundings as often as my surroundings collapsed or fell apart. Those days the dads on my block drank and fought with their wives, parents would be impulsive and call in their sons for punishment. The "two men" who lived across the street from me could get into heated arguments that usually led to some public altercation in their driveway. My mom told me they were uncle and nephew, but no uncle and nephew I knew spent that much time together alone. When my mom had discovered that I went to their house to look at their exotic fish tank, she freaked out and told me never to go there again. I was puzzled by her intense reaction, but years later I learned that my mom knew they were a same-sex couple, and I suspect she feared that they would molest me, she a victim to every gay stereotype in the books. Quite simply, to her, if they were gay, they were dangerous and living in sin.

Her maternal instinct to keep me safe meant that I, for a time, would interpret the world through her eyes. My dad kept his silence, but other voices provided a fatherly moral code: either the pastor or the conservative radio jockey Bob Grant. Once when I dropped my copy of Rush Limbaugh's newest book, my dad smiled. Rush's extreme conservatism helped me fit in both at home and in a world I did not belong to. I was everyone's kid, but no one's responsibility. I had three sister-moms, my brother and my parents. Plus I had God, Jesus and the Holy Spirit. I had lots of bosses and evolved into a sponge-like kid who absorbed it all.

In school, Samuel was a presence to me, but I steered as clear of him as humanly possible. I was more masculine than Samuel; at least I could hide my interest in boys to the point that Susan Grisly could confidently force her hand down my pants and expect no objection if not appreciation. Samuel couldn't hide his obvious homosexuality; the kids wouldn't let him. He was outed every day, mostly publicly. He was not allowed to be himself. They terrorized him, and they assailed me. The boys would physically abuse Samuel, punching him in the stomach, or keep basketballs from him during recess. He just wanted to play with them. With me, girls like Darla Sedgwick teamed up with the likes of Susan Grisly and Carmela Montefiore to berate me, or call me fat, or call my parents terrible names.

Overtime Samuel and I started talking. During one marking period, we were grouped together. Our desks sat across from each other or side-by-side. Ultimately, our victimization had brought us closer together. We would become each other's Good Samaritan more than we at the time knew. It would take years, some therapy, and later the Jesuits, to help me realize that religion was not simply about morality and ethics, that such was a naïve understanding of religion. Faith is about human relationship and human flourishing. When one is victimized as Samuel and I were, one does not flourish as part of the group called humanity; therefore one's flourishing is impeded if not ended. Children imitate their parents, they listen to the tales they tell; thus, Samuel and I couldn't flourish because our peers had been brought up by adults who had passed on negative values to them, not true Christian values of love and acceptance, so their children had no hesitation in outing Samuel as gay and me as a misfit. They needed us to fulfill these social roles.

In the eighth grade, when I was an altar boy, I had a budding faith as well as an ever-emerging understanding of my sexuality. Samuel and I started hanging out together after school. I was surprised by this turn of events, but I had just lost my circle of friends Matthew Gallagher, George Spinella, and Simon Booth to hip-hop and rap and weed. Matthew Gallagher was my best friend at the time, and the end of our friendship had devastated me. I turned to Samuel because I felt lost, and who better to ask to hang out than the one person I knew had nothing to lose.

It was about this time that grunge music and Nirvana was making their case for America's favorite music and best band, forever influencing the fashion and the music industry. I had hair like Kurt Cobain, the lead singer of the Seattle alternative rock band. I loved songs like *Smells Like Teen Spirit, All Apologies, Bleach* and *Pennyroyal Tea*. Their lyrics, along with those of Pearl Jam, Soundgarden and Alice-N-Chains, left me fixated on the present, helping me to ruminate on the way things are and should be.

My favorite song was *God* by Tori Amos, how she so rightly got the truth about God not coming through at times. I felt like the bare-chested teen boy in the MTV music video for Pearl Jam's top-10 song *Jeremy*. It was a song about a misfit boy, who longed to be a part of his community, his family and his world. I embraced that song, as much as I pined to be with a boy like the kid who played "Jeremy" in the video, his hairless chest, his nipples. He was a misfit who gained wisdom, and knowledge; Pearl Jam even referenced Genesis in the music video. Sometimes I'd feel out of breath while watching that video. "Jeremy" reminded me of a boy I knew from Memorial Junior High School-Jack Spalding. I was so happy to sit near Jack in Ms. Mantel's ninth grade English class, when he left school I lost my crush.

Samuel and I were very hyper adolescents with tons of repressed emotional energy stored up, energy stemming from our wounds, our being bullied, my dad's alcoholism or his being called "faggot." We had no outlet for our energy, so we'd play-fight, wrestle our dogs, wrestle each other, or I'd wrestle with his younger brother Peter. I had a crush on Peter the moment I saw him. I loved his luscious lips and his dimples, but nothing ever came of us.

Because I was never allowed to have Samuel in my bedroom, where I had most of my games and music, I moved everything to our basement where we also wrestled. We both got hard and turned on, and our hands ended up in each other's sweat pants. First, we lay on top of each other, slower to move off each other than usual; next we were side by side, looking at the white drop ceiling. My basement was dingy, and the boiler was running. It was winter, and there was fresh snow outside. It might have been a no-school day because of the snow. Then slowly but surely our hands moved from our sides, through the elastic waste of our sweatpants, past our pelvis, past our fresh pubic hair. Our hands were cold, and our breathing less forced. It was a strange feeling, holding Samuel's erect penis and scrotum for the first time. His penis seemed bigger than mine, and we just lay there for what seemed an eternity. I didn't look at his penis, nor did he see mine. Not that very first time. We didn't masturbate or whack each other off. Instead, it was our secret that was out, and in an instant Samuel removed his hand, he looked at me and I at him. Perhaps he felt my guilt, that I had felt like I had sinned; perhaps he saw the fear in my eyes and couldn't bear it. Surely this must have been the first same-sex sexual experience for both of us. Suddenly Samuel ran, he ran up the stairs and out my house's side door. I followed him in tow. He stopped momentarily, made a snowball, threw it at me, hitting my house, then called me a "shithead" and ran off.

I was immediately racked by guilt and needed to confess what had just happened, but it wasn't Saturday and I didn't know how to call a priest for confession. I called my newly certified and psychologically trained sister Anne. What I didn't know at the time was that Anne was steeped in the tradition of behaviorism and cognitive behavioral therapy. I lay on my bed and prayed for a moment, and when I had built up the courage, or perhaps from a sense of desperation or impulsivity, as the child of an alcoholic so often feels, I called my sister Anne in tears. She said, "What happened?" I told her everything about Samuel and me. I said, "Promise me you will not tell my mom. Promise." She said she wouldn't, but for some reason, I didn't trust her. Anne said she understood, "Don't worry about it, Benny." "Benny" should have been a clue. No one called me Benny.

We ended our talk, and I went to the washroom, composed myself, then returned to my bed and stared at the wall. I grabbed the Odie doll, from the cartoon Garfield that my sister Elizabeth had given me to sleep at night. I used it when I had nightmares about Freddy, or when my radiator hissed, or when my dad was in an alcoholic rage, and I wanted to forget everything. Then my mom called me. I crawled down the stairs, they cricked and creaked with each step, and when I got halfway down, I saw that my youngest sister Catharine was with my mom. That's when my mom and sister stormed at me, "Do you want to be a faggot?," and "You will burn in hell!" I forget what else they said, those words were enough. It felt like a chorus from a song, so powerful, so memorable, so consonant. I wept and all I could say was "yes," "no," then I ran up the stairs and slammed my door, and I cried myself to sleep.

Of course, their reaction was a Catholic imbued one: I was a sinner. God condemned me, and so they condemned me too. How ironic it is, now that I remember my young self, that I retreated for safety reasons further into the Church and my religion, the very Church that rejected me as a gay person.

Thoroughly confused and still reeling from my parents' rejection, I started using gay porn as well as having sex with Samuel, mostly oral sex. At first, being fastidious, I didn't want Samuel's cum in my mouth and would spit it out right away. I was the priority, because the more sex I had with Samuel, (anal sex came later) the more alive I felt. But sex was an escape, from self-pity, self-alienation, self-loathing and self-doubt, an escape from everything that made me feel like shit. If it weren't for this sexual release, I don't know how I would've gotten through this rough time. People often don't understand that sex, even my use of gay porn when I was alone, was a release from the self, a self-forgetting if only for a brief time. And I needed release often.

I also wanted to date Samuel because I longed for something beyond our physical, carnal appetites, but he refused. He wouldn't even kiss me. I thought a more emotional attachment between us would enkindle in me a liking for the sexual nature of our friendship. I remember writing him notes about this in school, secretly passing them to him because I feared that people might see that we were "together." Or far worse, catch them and read them or publish them. I was the one who passed; he was "gayer" or more out with every successive year, plus my faith led me into deeper conflicts. After every sex act I felt guiltier, certainly not a healthy feeling. At 40, I remain surprised by my younger self's lack of trust and courage when exploring my sexuality.

Soon first jobs came; I worked at Sears and Samuel at Starbucks. He dated other boys; I was deeply jealous, because I thought I loved Samuel, when I really needed him because with him I could be myself. Alone, I had to face conflicts caused by deep seated homophobia and anti-gay theology at home and at Church. Further, I envied Samuel's confidence, his parents "support." There was nowhere that I could be gay and happy.

About this time, my associate pastor from the Church of the Blessed Sacrament, Fr. Abraham Pardoen, informed me that he was convinced that I had a vocation to be a priest. He saw me teaching CCD on Sunday and after school, and he knew me from the liturgy and the brief conversations we had after mass. He observed piety, goodness and holiness in me, knew that I was becoming a Eucharistic minister, and he said, that I think you have a vocation to be a priest. He said, that a young man like me, one who was so active in the Church, had something special going on inside, and that it might mean that I was being called to be a sacramental priest. Soon I was working at the rectory as well as at Sears. Two jobs kept me in the money. Sears also provided me with a great opportunity to work with African-Americans, Latinos, and Central Americans, which provided me insight into discrimination and injustice, in a sense working in my suburban mall developed a cosmopolitanism in me. I also learned about rap and hip-hop from my bandstand mate Jamal Kirkland, an African-American who played saxophone alongside me in the high school band. We spent four years side-by-side playing Jazz, Sousa's marches and songs from Broadway, and to Jamal I was artsy, but not gay (I hadn't come out to anyone).

I was haunted by different voices and images and had to negotiate so many diverse interests through several lenses. I actually desired to be more effeminate, more "gay," thinking it would be easier for me to meet teenage boys. I thought, what if I were born a girl?

I lusted after Rick Steele and Nathan Sperrywood. Samuel and I lusted after a boy named Pablo, who lived in Syosset. Samuel had met him online, in the chatroom LongIslandm4m18to24. Pablo spent time with us together, and each of us alone. I feared Samuel might move on, but in reality he had already moved on. I accepted the fact that I needed Samuel far more than he needed me. Without him I don't know what would have happened to me. Turning to Jesus wasn't enough, because I had so much to fear. I feared the future, feared going away to school, feared leaving my mom at home alone with my alcoholic and depressed dad. Yes, I had a relationship with Jesus, but my trust in him had been so rattled by so many anxieties. And for the first time, I experienced doubt, that is, I weighed the benefits of flourishing in relationship with God or by seeking happiness through material possessions and secular humanism.

I admit to entertaining suicide, this intrusive thought came and went. I thought if God didn't make it easier for me by making me more effeminate then I could take the easy way out and end my life. If I were dead, I wouldn't be burdened by evil, sinful thoughts, *e.g.*, thoughts that led me to masturbate, to gay porn or finally to desire anal intercourse with Samuel. If I had only known that such things were natural rites of passage for both straight and gay boys, I wouldn't have been so desperate. I was imbued with the Catholic teaching of sin. So much guilt for such normal thinking and acting! Even the confessional stories of Saint Augustine and the Trappist monk Thomas Merton couldn't assuage my guilt; they weren't frank about sex or their sexuality. I had no Catholic heroes or lives of the saints to identify myself with.

Years later I'd also understand my feelings of guilt and anxiety to be part and parcel of my own symptoms of depression. I prayed through this first spiritual "desert moment." From such dryness I prayed to God to rescue me through Jesus Christ. It's rather paradoxical that when I was most spiritual, I was also most worldly. I partied, started to drink, and I then fell into not eating at all. I was in fact an anorexic. And to this day, I am still baffled by my anorexic behavior. Because I was a practicing gay, which was to my family and church sinful, was I by not eating hoping to disappear? What I should have done was stand before the mirror in my bedroom and remind myself that God loved me, that God created me beautifully, saying, to be gay is to be beautiful, over and over until I believed it!

Gay people my age met people on the Internet. We were a decade or so before "Coming Out" was all the rage. I met men in LongIslandm4m18to24. I had to give them my stats, and meet them in public places. We'd swap photos, I never sent nudes. I was too much of a prude. The conversations frustrated me enough, but they also gave me an outlet. Much like porn, they offered me a release from my inner and outer worlds. I sought comfort in human touch. I was a person both spiritual and sexual, neither ruling out the other. What I needed was to achieve a balance of the spiritual and the sexual. And I had a long way to go before figuring this out.

As high school ended, I wondered who I would be: a celibate gay man pushed to the margins by my Catholic family or a spiritual man who pursued priesthood with his Church, a Church whose vocation promoters and seminarians never spoke about sex, sexuality, or human intimacy during meetings about entering formation for the Diocese of Long Island. I was an actively gay man whose family would not approve of his "lifestyle" and would rather see him dead? I was an aloof loner who would succumb to his inner demons, and would often turn against himself. But, the root of suicide was not an option. Samuel helped me, and my faith-life comforted me. I would not go this route.

I was the president of the Environmental Club, selling tons of sweet and sour candy to raise money for the environment, traveled to Paris, published a poem and decided to attend Marist College, a Catholic college located in New York State. My college application essay was on "Ready-to-Assemble Furniture"; the *New York Times'* journalist Frank Bruni would have been happy, more importantly, it was a big hit with my senior year English teacher, Mr. Malcolm Boyd. Marist College was my mom's top choice, and I decided to go there because I had too many other things to balance. Choosing to be an openly gay priest did not cross my mind at this time because it didn't seem a possibility.

I left high school having dated, and loved the only woman I had sexual intercourse with, Samantha Beautiful. She was Russian Orthodox, an attractive, blonde haired, blue eyed woman with a female soccer player's build. She was generous, artsy, playing the flute, and intelligent. Both our families were from Maspeth, Queens. Our families bonded naturally. Our love was real, and mutual, but as she knows today, our love was doomed because I'm gay. I was, perhaps, using her in order to pass as straight for my parents' sake, to get them off my back, to keep things "cool" at home. We were generous to each other, I bought her gold jewelry from Sears, and she took us to see The Dave Matthews Band at Jones Beach. I am full of gratitude for her place in my life, and I shudder to think that our relationship wasn't authentic, as genuine as a gay man like me could offer her, a Platonic combination of Eros and Philia.

My first published work came in the form of poem placed in our high school yearbook. It was 1998. It was an untitled poem that went like this:

> We have walked these *stairwells*
> and talked through our years
> never knowing, never dreaming
> that one day we'd be gone.
> Off to the New World
> like Columbus and his ships
> We thought we knew our destiny
> and then we walked the *stairwells*.
> So many steps in our journey
> so many hellos and good-byes
> never dwelling on returning
> once we have gone.
> Who will remember
> the days in which our journey

dealt us hope and peace of mind—
so I ask you my brothers and sisters
not to linger on these *stairwells*
but to keep on moving right along.
Where we'll never see the *stairwells*
block us from our goals
where we'll never see the *stairwells*
keep us from our dawning
in the New World yet to come.

The poem speaks about my understanding of hope, hope for me as a young gay Catholic man in a world straight and heterosexist. As I left high school, I was full of hope, that wherever I would go, I'd always remember the past but not let it haunt me. I hoped that college might be a place where I'd continue to find myself. I also hoped that whatever plans God had for me, whether to be a priest or to be a gay man with a husband, that He would continue to guide me. But mostly I hoped that I wouldn't feel so lonely, so un-welcomed by my faith, by my family. I wanted to be welcomed into my home in a manner like that of the Prodigal Son, who when he began to ask his dad for forgiveness, he was stopped for there was nothing to forgive! But first I had to leave home to enter the unknown, and I soon found myself along the Hudson River, in Poughkeepsie, New York.

Chapter 4

Life along the Hudson

As MY DEPARTURE DATE for Marist College neared, I did the usual last minute checks. I went to Ikea, bought a down comforter, a lamp, a husband pillow (when I wanted a boyfriend!), and posters for my new dorm room. The lines at the Swedish owned minimalist themed store were long and nerve wracking; the parking lot, organized in such a convoluted way, frustrated buyers and elicited acute anger if not road rage in drivers. Still, going to Ikea in Hicksville was part and parcel of this collegial rite of passage. I chose muted colors like black or navy blue, not wanting to give away my interests in fashion and color to Brian, my soon-to-be straight college roommate and crew teammate.

By August, 1998, I had experienced the freedom of getting to know myself more intimately, for had I not been taught that self-knowledge was the greatest virtue, that on Greek temples blazed, "Know Thyself." I became acutely aware of my flaws, both psychological and physical. I was still struggling with accepting my being gay; I was also not pleased with my body, the latter still plagued by imperfections like scabby skin, wounds, and zits. I hadn't yet understood that my experience was not a one-of-a-kind one but universal, for I was also part of humanity, and we all share in the beauty of being human, although we often don't see the beauty, only the flaws.

As a teen I hated zits. I picked and picked at them, sometimes they would turn to scabs on my face. To me, it was a psychological release; if I picked enough at my skin, my worry about being a young, gay Catholic away from home would diminish or disappear. My obsessive worries also picked at me, the last child to depart from home, leaving my mom and dad in their torment, addictions and neediness.

By picking at my skin, I was picking at my fear of leaving Samuel Beckett behind, and charting a new course with new, unknown young men like myself, men who might not be as patient and gentle with me as Samuel was during sex. I fully understood that it would be difficult to find someone to replace Sam, and this turned more and more into an anxiety, one that likely caused my skin to break out, for I also learned in high school about psychosomatic illness. The skin on my face, for those with eyes to see, was the map of my mind and soul.

My family, especially my sisters, noticed my facial scars, but rather than seek the cause of the mauling of my face, which of course was psychological, they simply said, "Stop, messing up your face" and "Go to the Dermatologist." I'm convinced they knew the cause of my acne. They knew about my sexuality, and they knew I deeply felt their rejection. In fact, I knew that as a gay man I was anathema to them. What brother wouldn't be plagued by a skin disease? And I wondered, was I in some way buying into their opinion of me, subconsciously causing my skin to break out? Had I considered my face a portrait of my soul à la Oscar Wilde's Dorian Gray?

As the days of August wound down, I left my job at Sears, a job that I would work during every break in college. My mom never let me travel during spring break. In regard to money, Sears was generous; at 18 I was allowed to purchase stocks. I must admit I loved that job; it was fun, though I wished my parents would've been more culturally enlightened, by encouraging me to backpack in Europe before heading off to college. My parents encouraged me to keep busy, to stay out of trouble, to work now and to play later. But they didn't practice what they preached, for they steered clear of doctors, despite my mom's having gestational diabetes, which continued after I was born, and my dad having major depression. I wasn't allowed a sick day in high school, my parents often sent me to school sick: "Have an orange" and "keep busy" was the Brenkert *get well* model.

Towards the middle of August, I had worked up the courage to tell my best friends Samuel Becket and Leonicio Corona that I was thinking about becoming a Catholic priest. By then my family had known, for I informed them that I felt God was calling me to become a Catholic priest. While my family was relieved, as if scales had fallen from my eyes, Samuel and Leonicio were less convinced. Samuel, who had helped me to recognize and come to terms with my sexuality, and Leonicio, who had been my agnostic, non-practicing Catholic friend, looked at each other, a look of disappointment but their faces also said: Go, and find your self! Then we passed around a marijuana joint and started drinking Coronas. To us this was a celebratory act, and also, I now understand, an important rite of passage: I was just taking another step on that journey to self-knowledge. Needless to say, we got very high and drunk.

That summer I wasn't doing anything but thinking about the future, working, looking at gay porn (using a dial up connection), drinking and getting high. There were nights Leonicio and I would spend sipping coffee and eating donuts at Dunkin' Donuts. We'd stay there until 2 am, exhausted, sharing stories and dreams. I'd order the biggest coffee, he'd order a small hot chocolate and some donut, like a chocolate glaze. We'd rap up our conversation, hop in Al's Silver Bullet, which was becoming more and more *my* car, and drive home. Leonicio never drove; still to this day he doesn't have his license.

As I packed for freshman year, I'd often become nostalgic and sentimental. I'd go through pictures of Samantha Beautiful and me, or find mixed tapes with songs from The Smashing Pumpkins, The Grateful Dead or Dinosaur Jr. on them. I'd pull out my yearbook and read through notes from teachers, recalling the time I saved my Spanish teacher Ms. Madero from snow tubing into a fence during a school trip to the Camelback resort in Pennsylvania. I found notes from Samuel, pictures of me wearing Esprit jeans and shirt, too skinny for an 18-year old. I laughed over *The Elf Manifesto*, a short James Joyce-like essay, in which I narrated Edward-the-Elf's longing to put the Merry back into Christmas. My friend Kara Karing loved this story.

Then one hot and humid August day, I found myself staring at myself in my parent's new bedroom half-bathroom. It had enough room to stand and turn around, and it helped reduce the wait for the upstairs bathroom. In the image reflected back to me I saw a young man, whose scars and scabs were not going away, who still didn't possess the authority or the power to say: to be gay is to be beautiful. I grabbed a bottle of peroxide, and rather than tending to the scars of my acne, I used the entire bottle to dye my hair!

I had wanted to dye my hair for the longest time, to have the brightest blonde locks, to arrive at Marist College and be noticed for who I was on the outside, even though the person on the inside was so utterly confused, entirely homesick and afraid. As the peroxide went onto my hair, it also seeped into my scalp, it burned, and tingled, and smelled. My mom called out to me, "What are you doing?"; thankfully the door had a lock. I said, "I'll be out soon."

My hair turned from ash or dirty blonde to orange. Not an attractive color orange, perhaps the color of a rusted terracotta pot. After 15-minutes I left the bathroom, and my mom with utter shock gazed at me, her mouth open. I could see that she realized, perhaps for the very first time, that her control over me would begin to decline. My going to college, my becoming myself in another place than home, must have been like a nightmare for her, as it must be for any parent whose child leaves the safety of home to go into the world. Why the fear? Because the world, which can be so beautiful and exhilarating, can also be a cruel place, and I intuitively knew my parents feared for me.

The language that comes from out of the pain of discovery is not a predicament or paradox, but rather the grammar of a common experience known as being human. It is the experience of every human being, that at one time or another they will go into the woods, where if we're lucky, we learn how to be resilient, to trust ourselves, and to value our instincts.

I remember several details about my move to Sheehan Hall, the freshman dorm at Marist College. I remember the crowds and the parents; I remember shyer kids looking down in embarrassment while their parents decorated their rooms. I remember not wanting my older parents to do anything, lest they get injured. I remember meeting Calvin, my freshman RA, a tall, brown-eyed English-looking type, whose look back at me confirmed that I had "Gaydar," and I sensed that he really was attracted to me. I got my dorm key, then I opened my dorm room and found Brian, sitting in a recliner chair, playing Nintendo 64. The room had become his. I looked him over, head-to-toe, all 6 foot 1 inch and 200 lbs of him, and noticed that his bare-feet had toe fungus. I dry heaved. I knew that this smelly-jock and I would surely not get along; we had nothing more in common than being recruited for the Marist crew team. I found out later that Brian's uncle was an assistant coach.

As I started to complete the move and set up my side of the room, the day wound down, and my parents and I went off to lunch at what would become our favorite Italian restaurant, Route 9's Umberto's. We had a great meal, and it hit me then, that within hours I'd be alone on campus. I was overcome with anxiety. I felt as if I could cry at any moment for any reason.

After lunch, we went back to campus, and I thought, "Can I do this college thing?" I wouldn't hear my dad's verbal tic or read his mind. I wouldn't be around my mom, whose intimacy and love I still wanted more than anything else in the world. Samuel had already moved on, he had found a boyfriend (to me forgettable).

Before my parents drove off in my brother's Ford Explorer, we said our goodbyes. My mom and I said, "I love you." These three words between mom and child are sacred. I saw tears in my dad's eyes; he couldn't say anything more than, "Be happy and live one day at a time." That was his deepest advice. He himself had tried to practice that mantra in all of his affairs. As I walked back up the "Sheehan Hill," back to the dorm room, I felt desperately homesick, alone and uncertain. Before my first night at college ended I snuck down to the Hudson River, there by myself I wept miserably while watching the fireworks for new students explode. This is how my young adult life at Marist College, along the Hudson River started.

These were the days before every teenager had cell phones. I had ended the contract I had with my beeper. I'd no longer use beeper code to communicate with my friends, *e.g.*, using 07734 (Hello) or 143 (I Love you). I did use AOL, and Marist who partnered with IBM used Ethernet cables, which meant instantaneous access to Internet. No dialup introduced me to a fast-paced world without the interruption of incoming phone calls. Which also meant that I could download pornographic movies and develop interests beyond Gifs and Jpegs. Before long I met the Eastern European men who made the gay porn company Bel Ami famous, men like Johan Paulik or Lucas Ridgeston, moguls in the porn business. It didn't take long for porn to become one of my coping mechanisms for my homesickness. And, of course, it was a help in relieving sexual tension, for without Samuel, I was without a partner. And then, to be frank, porn, though many could dispute it, can teach one about sex, for imagining sex is one thing, seeing it is another, and I had many misconceptions cleared up by watching porn.

Now that I was away from home, I wondered, "Can I tell people at this conservative, Catholic campus, that I'm gay?" I also wondered if I should major in medicine, psychology or fashion merchandising. And I entertained new desires like should I try to have sex with my RA. And I began thinking about getting a job because I desperately needed money. All of this was swirling through my mind, so I can't say I was in any way calm, far from it. But what young guy that age is calm?

Again, money is always at the top of the list of my worries. And I liked money, having it and spending it. I pondered job possibilities. I knew that there was a Catholic Chaplain on campus, who ran ministry out of Our Lady Seat of Wisdom chapel. He'd surely need an assistant, or a sacristan. All too quickly I landed a job with Fr. Lyle McPherson, the Chaplain on campus, he was also a professor in the Religion Department.

I was to start at weekday mass that week, and I would be one of the three sacristans/chaplain assistants. I was so happy to get this job. It meant good pay, more than I expected. Earning money, discerning my call to the priesthood, settling into college life, being gay, I felt as if I were Jacob wrestling with God, as well as wrestling with myself with all my longings, dreams and anxieties. I could say I was a total mess, but I wasn't. I was simply a young guy with a life, so the dismissal "Get a life" wouldn't apply to me. And I accepted the fact that in life I'd have to face inner demons, but I had faith that I'd also have along the journey, angels.

I also realized that I was discerning between two goods: between being actively gay and partnered, and being a celibate, gay Catholic priest. Two goods, yes, but they also caused conflict because the Catholic Church condemns homosexuality. I'm gay, and I want to become a priest. Is this possible? And if not, how can I get around it? To be gay in the secular world is difficult enough, but to be gay in the Catholic Church for someone like me is more than difficult, it's a tremendous dilemma! It's something far worse than the quackery known as conversion or reparative therapy. As I walked home from Kirk House (where Fr. Lyle lived on campus) that August night I asked myself: Who am I? Who will I become? Thus, my dance with my identity and its many pirouettes had commenced.

I quickly learned about my job as sacristan, where I'd first set up the chapel for weekly mass, the altar, the chalice, the cruets, the missal, the hosts, all these were my responsibility. I would then be joined by some of the remaining Marist Brothers who live on the campus or nearby, as well as Fr. Lyle for the rosary. The Brothers were aged, pious, especially Brother Peter, who was as white as a ghost, who breathed heavily, likely suffering from respiratory ailments. Brother Peter was a former president. There was also Brother Jim who spoke French and bonded with me once when he learned that I was discerning a vocation to the priesthood. He was a cultured man, a bohemian, lost to the confines of the campus. I always imagined Brother Jim's looking out over the Hudson River from his penthouse apartment in Champagnat Hall and composing poetry in French, poems that caught the changing leaves and seasons, the iced-over Hudson, the panoramic sky, its cloud-islands floating by, a place far from the Eiffel Tower, but whose beauty demonstrated the triumph of God's design for creation, or as the Jesuit poet Gerard Manley Hopkins writes, "the world is charged with the grandeur of God."

Once, after mass, when I was ringing the bells, I struck up a conversation with Fr. Lyle about the priesthood. Since I had enrolled in his dreaded 8 am class on the Bible, where we were studying the royal priesthood of Melchizedek and his blessing of Abram in the Book of Genesis, I thought why not broach the subject. He looked back at me with his deep blue eyes nestled in wrinkles. I asked him if he would do it over again, i.e., being a priest. His response surprised me, "No, I'd be driving a red corvette, a convertible, and next to me would be a blonde bombshell, with long hair." He then said, "Ben, that's what you need."

I suspected that he was telling me something about his own loneliness, his own solitude. To him human touch is an obvious need, and had I known more about the poet Anne Sexton ("Touch is all"), we could've struck up a conversation about gesture, touch, memory, perhaps even debated why priesthood was mutually exclusive of falling in love or sexual intimacy. Yet,

Fr. Lyle never stayed put for long, likely racing home to care for his older sister who lived with him in Kirk House.

I had wanted to tell him I was gay, to tell him about my love of Jesus, but I sensed it wasn't the right time to come forth with this information about myself. Of course, there was the fear that he'd not understand me. If my own family couldn't understand me, how could I expect understanding from a priest I'd just met!

When I wasn't in the chapel praying, or working, I was in class, suffering anxieties about my transition, as well as from hangovers. My first semester was not going well because I was a mess, plagued by so many conflicting feelings about myself; on one hand I accepted my being gay, but on the other an inner voice chastised me for it, saying maybe the church is right in condemning homosexuality. But then another voice would fight back: God made me this way, and He loves me for who I am. This back and forth of alternating voices was going on all the time. Thank goodness I had befriended Michelle, a hot, model-type, who suffered from anorexia, and whose boyfriend would visit from time to time. I left the Marist crew team, but met my best friend Marlon Aquila, a Central American transplant who immigrated to the states illegally. Marlon was an attractive, sensitive individual, and girls flocked to him for his charm and light brown skin as much as for his ability to hold a conversation and dance at the local club McCoy's. Girls were also interested in hooking up with me, but I just played it off. I could've had my fair share of sex with the opposite sex that fall, but I was attracted to my own sex, so I allowed my sexual identity to affirm itself. Of course, my pretending to be straight wouldn't be fair to any girl. I needed to allow this integration, or I would've been a greater mess than I was.

At midterm my grades sucked. On learning about my turmoil at college, my mom threatened to take me home, "Shape up or else." I did shape up. I got my act together. I learned how to cope, how to drink; to stop when I was on the verge of being drunk.

I had no gay friends. My RA Calvin and I had a falling out over my interests in a senior, a theatre student named Kyle Boring. Kyle cantered at the Sunday night student mass, something that a gay man could do then without worrying that the Church might fire him. He was from upstate NY, had effeminate features, drove a then famous Dodge Neon, and was in a relationship with his then roommate Rodney Adamant. Rodney was the dominant male type, and treated Kyle like shit. Kyle took it all, because, I surmised, he loved Rodney, especially when Rodney took to flicking me out of the picture. I somehow threatened Rodney. When I saw Kyle and Rodney at mass that year, Kyle gave me that deeply regretful look, the "If circumstances were different we'd be together."

I wanted a lover. And I finally realized that I had a lover: Jesus Christ. This stunning realization brought me closer and closer to Him. I begged God to let me meet a normal guy on this crazy, conservative campus. Let me meet a guy who's not conflicted, not fucked up, a guy who would love me for who I am—as He does. But there was no one on the horizon. I needed Christ to be sure, but I couldn't put my arms around Him, I couldn't cradle His head in my hands, I couldn't kiss Him. And He couldn't do the same for me. I needed a man *in carno*!

I could no longer turn to Samuel, for he had a new boyfriend, Varian. With no one in my life, I retreated to gay porn and the Internet, to drinking, and to excessively working on schoolwork. I stayed at the library until all hours in the morning. I became more and more depressed, alienated an achingly lonely.

My sophomore and junior years passed rather quickly. I had a nice group of straight friends; I was in the Marist Band, playing saxophone through all four years of college. I was now the Chaplain's Assistant, Fr. Lyle had been replaced by a neo-conservative, diocesan priest, Fr. Robert Ladue. He and I became friends, and he increased my responsibilities at the chapel and in campus ministry, all to the chagrin of Brother Fred Knight. Brother Fred, a rotund, grumpy Marist Brother, who hung out with frat boys late at night in his apartment, never liked me. He never liked that I spoke about the priesthood, or my wanting to become a priest. He didn't like when I gelled my hair, and he didn't like the way I dressed.

He wouldn't like knowing about the nights I snuck into the chapel, drunk, with my pals, and drank the altar wine, taking some of it back to our townhouse. He wouldn't like it that I rang the church bells drunk, wildly swinging on the rope because I had lost more weight and had little strength.

Over the years, college drinking had given me an outlet or rather an escape for my stored resentment, my loneliness, and my solitude. My drinking was concomitant with my increasing anger at my church: The Catholic Church wasn't changing her position on anything: birth control, communion for the divorced, abortion in special cases, gays and gay love.

As Pope John Paul II declined in health and the sex abuse scandal continued to rock the very foundations of the Church, Rome turned a blind eye to the needs of her people. And the Church refused to differentiate between pedophilia and homosexuality. In other words, gays were responsible for the pedophilia scandal. In other words, I was anathema. No wonder I drank!

I was so conflicted that I was sent to a Marist Brother, James Nice, for therapy. A write-up my freshman year for drinking-under-age on campus had forced me to register with him for treatment. He was what I would term an assimilationist. He wanted to help me find ways to blend in, to become part of the campus community, to disappear into the crowd and not to rock the boat. As I worked through therapy, I desired to become more confident, more self-assured, more able to intuit that God made me gay. And I also became more determined not to allow the Catholic Church to possess my soul at the expense of my being. I was fraught with ambivalence: Amo et odi, I love and I hate. The Church? Me?

Brother James introduced me to Marist's lesbian professor Joan Metz. Joan wore black, had Goth-like white skin, distinctly European features, and was strikingly beautiful. As a history major, I had often passed by her office, since she taught in the department of political science. I'd look in through the window of her office door, and when she wasn't there, I'd gaze at her mess of papers, her postings on the door. She had pink triangle stickers and rainbow magnets and a Human Rights Campaign equality sign: She eschewed the type of confidence of self that I so desired. I wanted to meet her, to learn from her, even if it were through some kind of osmosis. Brother James encouraged me to meet her. It was after all my senior year, and I was ready to meet my first lesbian! It sounds so naïve to say this, but the fact is I'd never met or known a lesbian, so it was in a sense adventurous, like entering *terra incognita*.

I enrolled in her classes, in part to fulfill my remaining requirements as a double major in American Studies and History. Professor Metz and I bonded immediately; by then I had been promoted to an Editor on the staff of the student newspaper, *The Circle*. I was charged with leading the Opinion Section. I promoted multiculturalism and pluralism; I challenged the whiteness of Marist's campus, its xenophobia, its heteronormativity and heterosexism. Even though I myself was still closeted, I wanted Marist, I wanted the Church, I wanted the world to become a far better place for LGBTQ youth, the people behind me. I longed for parents to let their LGBTQ children pursue their dreams, to become anything, from a ballet dancer, to a member of the U.S. Military, to a Roman Catholic priest.

I had finally started to learn the names of gay heroes like the historian Martin Duberman, or the politician Harvey Milk. I had been introduced to little, secret gay histories, like the Newport Sex Scandal, which I'd end up writing about for my thesis. My attachment to my Church and to the desire to be a priest was growing stronger. I saw the Church and the sacramental nature of the priesthood as a means to inclusivity, to helping the LGBTQ community become full members of society, a society well before marriage equality, or the free markets embrace of sexuality and gender equality and civil rights for LGBTQ people. I founded Marist's Gay-Straight Alliance.

When 9/11 happened, the world changed, and it would never be the same. America was attacked, white supremacy was attacked, empire and colonization were under siege. The Western world was on the alert against terror and terrorism, and people were called to become radically honest. For a brief moment, America's parents hugged their children closer and lovingly tucked them in tighter at night.

I too was deeply affected by 9/11. I had three family members working in New York, and when their cell phones went dead, I obsessed about their well-being and safety. In fact, I couldn't make any outgoing calls to them for the entire day. I sat in front of the television, with my housemates, all of us either just waking up or in different states of consciousness. We watched the smoke billow, we watched frame after frame of the planes hitting the buildings. Just beyond the television set, sat the Hudson River, flowing gloriously that morning, the sun bright, golden, reflecting her rays off the water and the hills. The trees green, but readying for fall; it was a gorgeous day made hideous by the events in lower Manhattan. As each tower fell, I thought about my family, I thought about my brothers and the community around me, I thought about the presence of evil in our world and what Jesus' death and resurrection might begin to mean now. As the smoke rose from the cremated site of the World Trade Center, I prayed for what had now become a cemetery. My relationship with God was close; I wondered about those that had no faith, and for whom faith would mean nothing in response to this merciless crime.

Then President George Bush told us to shop, to buy things, to "return to normal." How could anything ever be normal? I was sympathetic to everything *New York Times* columnist Maureen Dowd had said about him and his dynastic legacy. I refused to be "normal." I refused to remain ash, to die another day locked inside or to remain self-tortured by lying about my gay identity. That summer before our senior year, Marlon and I had gone out to a bar in Long Beach. When we returned to my home, we sat outside my house on Fir Street, in Valley Stream. I had been working up the courage to tell him about my sexuality, many years before I'd read Paul Tillich's *Courage to Be*, that wonderful book that would later exert such a positive effect on me.

He sensed that I had something to tell him, my nervousness giving me away. It was the first time I'd tell a non-high school friend that I was gay. I said I couldn't enter senior year without your knowing that I am gay. I trusted him. I emulated him by getting a cross forever tattooed on my back. Everything spilled out, when I first knew, my telling to friends and family, my hurts about being rejected by some, and by the time I was finished, I was drenched in sweat. He calmly listened, said nothing, but I could tell that he wouldn't reject me.

He asked me questions about my growing up, about school, about my family. He saw how conflicted I was about my religion, and he understood my anxiety about the conflict of my being gay, my religion and my wanting to be a priest. Then we hugged. Latino men are good for that; while they are masculine, they know about intimacy and the need for human touch.

Marlon knew that I'd be telling my housemates about my sexuality, that I planned to come out my senior year. I hated hiding, especially since I wanted to date men openly during my senior year. I was tired of porn, tired of clandestine meetings in mall parking lots, tired of being dateless, tired of driving past Vassar College, where I dreamed about some smart, blonde, twinkish college student who might be interested in me. A twink is a young, effeminate acting gay boy, age eighteen to early-twenties, who has little body hair, is slender and usually blonde haired and blue-eyed; is remembered for his outward appearance not his inner depth, i.e., pretty boy. Truth be told, I hadn't dated a man from 1998 until October 2001. I did date the Marist Brothers, even though religious life was always on my mind, though, of course, to my way of thinking one shouldn't preclude the other. The call to the religious life that began in the middle of my adolescence was hard to escape; it was even harder the more I believed how good, positive, real, trustworthy and loving was my relationship with God and his Son, Jesus.

I remembered Fr. Lyle's vision for himself driving in that red corvette, with the blonde bombshell. I more, fully understood, now what he meant; he was telling me to experience life to the full, to fall in love, to have fun, to experience human touch. If I were to become a priest, all of these experiences, all so human, would make me not only a better man but a better priest; furthermore, how could I as a priest ever help anyone if I had never had sex, had never been intimate, had never loved, had never experienced the full force, positive and negative, of life in general?

With 9/11 everyone's sensitivities were distilled; we felt the world differently, breathed in and out, prayed closer, experiencing community for the first time as Americans. I thought about George Washington and others sailing up and down the Hudson, forming a nation bonded by brotherhood. 9/11 was America's, and my own turning point.

That week I came out to my housemates. Their response was awesome, from Tim's comment that he'd kick anyone's ass that called me a homo or fag, to Demyan, my Russian housemate's response, calling me cool; he even started singing the then popular song *It Wasn't Me*, by the Hip Hop artist Shaggy, to even further lighten the mood and normalize the group's acceptance of me. That night I felt that I was blessed. I was full of gratitude; while my Church and my family thought I should become someone or something else, my friends accepted me for who I am, welcoming me even deeper into human relationship with them. Later, that night, after drinks with my buddies, I called my good friend Kimberly Serenity and shared the good news of my coming out story; the positive reactions by my peers helped me to believe even more that being Gay and Catholic was just a part of the whole picture of Benjamin James Brenkert, the young man God created on February 16, 1980.

Over the next few months, I blazed, brimmed with joy. I was full of confidence and inspiration. I had heard Benjamin Barber speak at Vassar College, started reading Immanuel Kant, Martin Luther King, Jr, Mahatma Gandhi, Michel Foucault, and Annamarie Jagose. I confronted injustice and discrimination in *The Circle*, taking on Marist's poster boy, the Fox journalist Bill O'Reilly. I confronted homophobia. Then, with one article, I lambasted Marist's treatment of LGBTQ students, calling it outright homophobic. I opined that any LGBTQ or non-religious student should not have to walk past a giant crucifix to meet their therapist. I strongly believed that to some of these students that crucifix meant that they were "demons," "disordered," "against nature" or far worse, better off dead. What they needed was an image of Christ's resurrection, or better yet a Church that accepted and loved them.

Having read my article, Fr. Robert Ladue called me immediately. I went to Kirk house, now a stone's throw from my townhouse. We met, I heard his fish tank gurgling; he had so many freshwater tanks and flowers. Fish were his friends, and flowers his children. He looked at me, seated on the couch across from him, his rage seething, his eyes icy.

I had never before seen his anger. It frightened me, I tried to diffuse the situation with humor, but he'd not have it. He was wearing his Roman collar; consequently, this was a conversation between priest and parishioner, not Robert and Ben, the college student. He said, "What the hell were you thinking?" I was dumbfounded. I then explained my article and the reasons behind it, which included a pursuit for justice. He still wasn't buying it. Then, I tried to take it to that place of personal narrative, speaking about a place that I'd learned by then that the Catholic Church would never go near, a discomforting place where supposed natural law possessed no answer, because we weren't talking about culture any longer; we were talking about God, and nature as God had made it. We were in the realm of nature, not culturally contrived nature, but existential nature, and what it means to be, to exist.

I attempted to come out, and Fr. Robert would've been the first priest I came out to. He picked up on my intent and wouldn't let me finish a sentence. I said, "I have something to tell you, I am—" when he cut me off. He said, "If you go any further, our relationship will change forever." What did he mean? And perhaps only a Catholic can understand how momentous this occasion was for me. Wearing his Roman collar, Fr. Robert represented the Church, in all her power, with all of her history of empire making. As a priest he also represented Christ on earth. If Christ were indeed in front of me and heard my declaration about being gay, He'd have embraced me, He who loved the Beloved John. The Beloved disciple, the only person to rest his head on Jesus' breast. But this priest who should have been a Christ to me was merely an ordinary man.

He said: You cannot be a gay man and a good Catholic. He affirmed again that to become a priest I'd have to be celibate, for sexuality had no place in the priesthood. And there was certainly no place for a gay man. I left his office, weeping.

That same year my mom stopped speaking to me after I came out to her at Thanksgiving. I had told her that I was visiting my boyfriend in Connecticut, a NYU student, and would spend a day or so with him before heading back to Marist. We had a heated exchange, and afterwards I grabbed my things and stormed out. Brother James knew I was planning to speak with her, but he knew she'd go into orbit. 9/11 had caused me to be anxious about time and space, and I felt none of us could put things off. But when was the right time for anything anymore?

Over time my relationships with mom and Fr. Robert stabilized. I cannot not say we reconciled. Yes, we loved each other, but it was not Agapetic Love for which there are no conditions. My mom loved me, but there was one BIG condition: she didn't want to hear about my sexuality or my boyfriends. My dad came to my winter band concert, bringing along my sister Liz. I looked around and was stunned to find that my mom had refused to come.

While my dad didn't speak much, his actions proved his unconditional love for me. And I shall always remember his loving presence at my college concert. And I will unfortunately remember my mom's absence. I don't mean to sound melodramatic, but I felt as if I'd been physically harmed, like being slapped or punched. My mom would never do the latter to me, but she unknowingly hurt me to the core of my being, because I loved her so much and wanted her to be with me. Her absence proved to me the negative affects of her St. Joseph's Baltimore Catechism formation, which included a spiritual malformation, and an expression of religion situated (rigidly) in a question and answer format, at the expense of the individual's development of a personal relationship with God, Jesus or the Saints.

The Yale University law professor, William N. Eskridge, Jr. writes, "Biblical support for slavery, segregation, [sodomy] and anti-miscegenation laws rested upon broad and anachronistic readings of isolated Old Testament passages and the Letters of Paul, but without strong support from Jesus' teachings in the Gospels." Slowly but surely the populist sentiment was challenging the status quo, that considered LGBTQ people as second-class citizens. Eskridge continues, "In his teachings, Jesus emphasized love for one's neighbor and tolerance for the many kinds of people in the world. Jesus instructed his followers, *Judge not, and you shall not be judged; condemn not, and you shall not be condemned.*" Jesus who called his Father *Abba* (daddy) favored diversity and pluralism.

Fr. Robert and I returned to our usual ways; he needed me to do what I did best, be a young, talented, energetic gay man who was employed (tenuously) by the Church to create prayerful space for worship and community. Had the Church recognized me for all of my talents? I'd say yes, but the Church wouldn't recognize me as a gay man. Sadly, today, so many LGBTQ employees and volunteers, like Colleen Simon and Nicholas Coppola, are being fired from the Church for doing the kind of thing I did and for being who they are.

Perhaps these frustrations, with my exile from home and Church, fed my discernment not to enter the Marist Fathers at the end of college. Perhaps these frustrations fueled my interest in working with LGBTQ youth as a clinical social worker. As such, I applied and accepted an offer of admission to CUNY-Hunter College's School of Social Work. That summer I landed a position in the New York office of then Senator Hillary Rodham Clinton; I felt like I was on top of the world.

Fr. Robert and I did our best to remain in relationship those final months, and somehow our friendship survived. I'm saddened that I couldn't be honest with him about myself, indeed, our relationship reminded me of the one I had with my Catholic family, our version of the U.S. military's "Don't Ask, Don't Tell" policy. There was an awkwardness, an unease, I finally had my bleached-blonde hair, spending my money at the local salon. I didn't need the Peroxide anymore; there were real professionals out there who'd give me the notorious rapper Eminem-styled locks. Like his song, *The Real Slim Shady*, I often wondered when, with Fr. Robert would the real Ben Brenkert be able to stand up.

Then graduation came, and the blizzard of May 2002 showered down rain, snow, ice and wind upon the many thousands who traveled to Poughkeepsie to see a son or daughter graduate. In many ways I went through college like a Blizzard, strident, idealistic, focused and confused. All of us graduates were sent to the McCann Recreation Center where we piled in with our families. Safe from the weather outside, we did our best to listen to NBC's journalist Gabe Pressman tell us about the road ahead.

The road ahead is just how Poughkeepsie was developed, first by water, then by train, then by car. Poughkeepsie whose poverty remains, and whose allure the Dutch meaning of her name captures, "The Queen City of the Hudson." While I did not find love at Marist, I did find bits of myself, and my many, many good college friends. Before long, I'd be back to Long Island, in New York City, one of the many interns working for "The Queen of the Senate," Hillary R. Clinton. I was filled with the courage to hope; as dramatist Lillian Hellman said, "It is best to act with confidence, no matter how little right you have to it."

As I embarked on my last drive home from Marist, that lump in my throat returned, I avoided the rearview mirror for a time, I tried to keep Al's Silver Bullet at an even 55mph. I thought about forgiveness and reconciliation, such crucial components to authentic Christian living. Forgiveness rests in the power of the victim. Forgiveness yields: 1) removal of hostility; 2) charity and compassion; 3) the possibility of apology and contrition; 4) re-integration of the evildoer into society; and 5) the promise of benevolent relationship based upon mutual recognition, respect, and human flourishing. Goods of forgiveness for the victim and for the perpetrator include mutual recognition and respect; both increased mutual recognition and respect promise new beginnings at the time of new dialogues about sameness and difference between individuals and groups.

But why would I, a gay man who strived to practice an authentic Christian life have to spend an entire lifetime seeking forgiveness and reconciliation if God made me in his image and likeness? Wouldn't that be like a tall person or a Polish person or Latino person seeking forgiveness and reconciliation for something they could not change: height, ethnicity or race. The Church practiced sexuality-blindness, attempting to inculcate a morality of hate the sin, love the sinner. Did she need LGBTQ people to fill her pews? Despite knowing this, I lived in tension, and brought such grievances to my discernment about being an openly gay priest.

It would be some years before I forgave my mom and Fr. Robert.

As blizzard like conditions on the road let up, the song *What it's Like* by Everlast came on the radio. I remembered my life along the Hudson River; I remained convinced that I would not be oblivious to the spiritual and material needs of LGBTQ people. I felt called to witness prophetically to their deprivation, and to confront the Church for her millennia of anti-gay theology and anti-gay rhetoric. One answer to the question, "How?" would come three years later when I'd enter the Society of Jesus in 2005.

Chapter 5

Hitting Rock Bottom

I MET THE JESUITS that final spring semester at Marist College. I wasn't discouraged by the negative press gays received from the sex abuse scandal. It was a myth that gays were pedophiles, for most pedophiles are heterosexuals who are stuck at an early age of sexual development. Of course negatively labeling gays as "pedophiles" is another way gays are an Othered group, hence scapegoats. As a consequence, gays are made hyper sexual.

I had gone online to www.nysj.org and printed everything I could find. When I passed the Culinary Institute of America, I thought about its being the site of training for novices, known as St. Andrew's on the Hudson. I thought about the Jesuits buried there, like Fr. Teilhard de Chardin whose *Hymn on the Universe* spoke about God's grandeur and the interdependent interrelationship between man and the world.

As I tore up the printouts, I thought, impulsively, the Jesuits will never accept me. This order is far too intelligent, far too erudite, far too cultured. Yet, our lives and stories had met along the Hudson River; it was as if the consciousness of de Chardin led me to be reunited with Christ in the Jesuits. Would the Society of Jesus become for me my *Divine Milieu*? Would it be the locus where I too could pray Chardin's prayer, "Grant, that I may see You, even and above all, in the souls of my brothers, at their most personal, and most true, and most distant."

My personal relationship with Christ had taken its toll my senior year of college. I was caught in the age-old, Augustinian trap of body versus soul. Fortunately, I possessed a healthier attitude toward sex than had Augustine, he who cried, "Lord, make me chaste, but not now." But sex and my frustrations interfered with my relationship with Jesus. I loved Jesus, and I believe He loved me, but I couldn't escape the feeling that I had let Him down—and this feeling did not originally come from me, it came from my Catholic conditioning: that one's being gay is intrinsically disordered, to have gay sex is sinful.

Later, St. Ignatius of Loyola would avail me the opportunity to work through these frustrations spiritually. An opportunity came during the preparation days of my thirty-day silent retreat when using his *Spiritual Exercises*, I would pray the Psalms of creation and learn to joy again in my created nature and ontological being. To joy in the words of Psalm 139,

> O LORD, you have searched me and you know me. You know when I sit and when I rise; you perceive my thoughts from afar. You discern my going out and my lying down; you are familiar with all my ways. Before a word is on my tongue you know it completely, O LORD. You hem me in—behind and before; you have laid your hand upon me.

In short, if anyone knew me, God did. Every inch of me, mind, body and soul, before time began, in and beyond time itself. And God accepted me, of that I was convinced. Acceptance by Holy Mother Church, well, that was another matter.

During this time, I never for a moment thought God was dead. While God did feel far and remote from me those first few months back at home, I went to mass, even daily mass when possible. I still believed that God works through groups and community, hence the creation of early Christian literature, like the Christian Testament's canonical Gospels.

But if my church doesn't accept me as a gay person, as a member in full communion (good standing) with the Church, she then is denying, if not destroying, my identity. Some would argue, why do you care if you're accepted or not? I care because I am a Catholic, my family is Catholic, and many of my friends are Catholic. Catholicism is in my bones, my DNA. And if the church in her ignorance rejects me, then I will do all I can to convince her to accept me and every other gay person in world. Not only to accept me, but to practice what Christ taught us, to love me!

Moreover, the Church endangers her gays by sending out the message that a gay person lacks the ability to fully flourish as part of the community and as an individual. The church excludes gays. If they live a gay life, they, according to the church, live in sin. They, therefore, cannot receive the sacraments, the Eucharist. Thus, we LGBTQ boys, girls, men and women (and now non-binary and gender fluid people) have been cast forth from the kingdom; we are the rejected, we are the condemned, we are not worthy to receive Christ in Holy Communion, but don't we all say at mass, "I am not worthy?"

Thus, I began my life as a post-undergraduate student, wondering: How should I respond to a Catholic world that defines me as a non-person? I further asked, in a Post-9/11 world why are gay priests so cowardly—what do they risk if they identify as gay: everything? To say the least, I had a lot on my mind, but this didn't dissuade me from my vocation to become a priest. I would learn as much as I could about the Society of Jesus because I felt called to become a Jesuit priest.

In May 2002, I started my internship in the office of Senator Hillary R. Clinton within days of my return home. I went to her Third Avenue office and met peers from Ivy League colleges and universities, like Cornell University and Columbia University. I worked with an attractive, rich, princess-type named Natalie Bretske and a privileged, somewhat well-connected guy named Kwami Underloo. We shared responsibilities in Clinton's department of intergovernmental affairs, which was the highest positioned placement for interns. We were charged with responding to grant requests. While I felt disadvantaged as a member of the middle-class, I was still able to bond with new friends, like the very Polish looking, though heterosexual and charming, Seth Piazza.

Seth and a college friend had rented a room near the World Trade Center. We lunched often, and he often complained about the "stupid shit" he had to do on the other side of Clinton's office. I told Seth about my application essay, about the need to reform society to account for the dignity and worth of every LGBTQ person, pointing out that it was government's duty to do so, noting also that the free market and Capitalism cannot be the sole corrective force that challenges the status quo and creates social change. I cited Martin Luther King, Jr.'s concept of the Beloved Community. It was as if James Baldwin's comment in his text *The Cross of Redemption*, "not everything that is faced can be changed, but nothing can be changed until it is faced" was written on my soul.

One night, Natalie, Kwami and I attended a reception hosted by President Bill Clinton. For me, it was a dream-come true, and I felt on top of the world. I had already met and felt the esteem, charm and charisma of Hillary, but now we were to meet her husband Bill. What a perk of this unpaid, government sponsored internship! The three of us worked late until the evening that hot summer day, then left with our supervisor, the very capable and very politically learned African-American Billy Small. When we got to the bar, it was packed, people in suits everywhere. It was so hot, the air conditioner clearly wasn't working. I watched as Natalie bought drink after drink. I didn't really know her, or her alcohol limit, besides everyone was having fun. Then Bill arrived, with his security detail. He passed through the crowd, vibrant, alive, a man who had survived scandal, a man who'd established a political dynasty with his wife, Hillary.

Hillary wasn't present, where was she? In any case, Bill came up to us, we told him who we were, and he said, "Fantastic, take care of my lady for me." He had such a cool southern accent. The next thing I remember is Natalie's falling to the floor, from a combination of too much excitement, too much heat and too many drinks. Bill assessed her condition quickly, and we scurried back to the office. Natalie got a firm talking to in a closed-door session with Bill. I never saw Natalie again that summer.

I'll never forget this experience. Learning a lot from it; I watched Bill Clinton take complete charge, saw his unflappable confidence, experienced his instant control of a situation. And I learned to take nothing for granted. One can be on top of the world but in an instant, one can topple. Good lessons for a gay person, for any person!

Back on Long Island, I had returned to Sears; unlike the other Clinton interns I had to keep busy and earn money. In doing so, I scaled back my hours at Senator Clinton's office. Thankfully, Bill understood. The money I made kept my tank in Al's Silver Bullet full, and it also afforded me the opportunity to pay cover charges for beers at New York's gay clubs. While I was home, and having put my discernment to become a Catholic priest temporarily on the back burner, I pursued what my mom called "an actively gay lifestyle." She, and my family still had no interest in where I went, nor could I bring men home. My mom, however, still sat up waiting for me to return home, sometimes at 2 am, other nights 4 am, and some nights not at all.

I'd enter the house, and there my mom was, sitting on her red, leather recliner chair in the dark. I loved my mom for her care and concern for me; I would always be her child, and my safety/wellbeing her principle concern; it was from my mom, in part, that I learned about the practical nature of Feminism's Ethics-of-Care.

One night I drove to Huntington to meet my gay, college friend from Marist. The powder-blue eyed, pale, blonde twink I had a crush on was James Messi. Once when I asked him out, he quickly shuffled me off to his friend. I was hurt, deeply, though I soon mended.

There we were, in one of Long Island's dumpiest gay bars, located in Huntington, near Syosset. That night I'd meet Jim Stephenson. Jim had jet black hair, deep brown eyes, built like a swimmer, and drank the Heinekens that I bought.

As our conversation went deeper, I couldn't help falling for him. We talked about our jobs; he was impressed that I interned with Senator Clinton. He was buying time between jobs in construction; he even had that landscaper, construction worker tan. We talked about where we lived; he was staying with a friend in New Hyde Park, but came from Riverhead. We talked about the music that was playing, how lame it was and how we made fun of "femme" gay men. Then he asked me to dance, and I was thrilled, loving every minute with him. Jim followed me to Al's Silver Bullet, and we sat in my car and talked. I could cut the sexual tension, and we finally kissed and passionately made out. I was thrilled that he liked me as much as I liked him.

I kissed Jim because I wanted human connection and human intimacy. He was a good, sensual kisser. I felt very alive while we locked our lips together. I understood what many people thought of men making love. I had heard the ugly comments, the epithets the curses. I knew many people had said that God had sent AIDS to punish men who had sex with one another. I, a sensitive, empathic, young conflicted gay Catholic man, wrote about these traits in my application essay to graduate schools of social work. I proved successful, as I was headed that summer to begin my career as a social work student at CUNY-Hunter College, not my first choice college but my inevitable choice because I couldn't afford the tuition at Columbia University or the tuition at New York University.

When that night Jim gave me his phone number, I was over the moon. Over the next month he and I did everything we could together. Our sexual appetites were simply part of our connection, both physical and emotional. Simply put, we really got along famously. I liked Jim, beyond well enough, but he didn't want to settle down into a long-term relationship.

I wanted him to date me exclusively. I joyed when we drove side by side in his blue Chevrolet pick-up truck. It felt good (sic normal) to be in relationship with Jim, making me feel free and alive. And while Jim and I danced at the Roxy with our shirts off, or sipped martinis and beers at G, we stayed away from places like the Limelight, but that did not stop us from trying threesomes with other men. In truth, I was only a month into New York's gay scene and I was exhausted. It required so much energy, stamina, money to drink and all my will power to turn down Ecstasy and Cocaine. I also had to muster more will to turn down sex in the backrooms, bathrooms and dance floors of clubs. All of this I could've chosen, but I saw how illusory it all was, very alluring to a young man, but not so much as to win me over, the greater lure being God and my someday being one of his priests.

Every time I removed my shirt, or passed up coke, I thought about closeted gay priests who don't see this because they aren't connected to it. I thought that God is not closeted, that God cannot be held back. I feared the destructive nature of a system that produced pedophiliac priests. Yes, we were still in the throws of the Church's sex-abuse crisis. To me, the Church was convoluted by her closeted God; by opposing the Incarnational nature of Christianity and thereby rejecting themselves, the silence of closeted gay priests unwittingly supported this process of dehumanization, diminishing, if not destroying the dignity and worth of gay people everywhere.

If I were to be a priest, I would refuse with all my strength to be closeted. I would be out no matter what. I wouldn't allow myself to be alienated from people by denying my sexuality. Thus, when I went out to dance, I allowed myself to release the hurt, pain, sadness and anger that had accumulated ever since I knew I was gay, most of it caused by my own church and her teachings, and, of course, by my family. My family was (mal)formed by the Church's teaching, perhaps then like other Catholic families their free thinking about gays is shaped by unchanging doctrine, dogma and a century old tradition that denies the Post-Modern world and tells its members, "there is no disagreement with Mother Church."

Jim helped me tremendously, but his not wanting a relationship frustrated me. One night I dragged my college friend Karissa Smallwood to Long Island's other gay club Luxe. It was a Wednesday night, and I needed a release from Jim, Sears and Hillary Clinton. Dancing offered me that release, and the opportunity of meeting someone else.

As I danced and locked lips with strangers on the dance floor, Karissa pulled me away and said there was a guy following me. I looked over and saw a petite, young man, a look-a-like for the American pop star Justin Timberlake. I was instantly attracted to him, but at the same time, his looks made me wary, and while my internal message read, "Stay away" Karissa said, "Go say hi." I did, reluctantly. Then my life changed forever.

I called Steven Dogwood the next day, from my basement, in the laundry room, near the boiler. I didn't want anyone to hear me ask him out. My bedroom still didn't have a lock on the door, which still meant I had no privacy. What was I hiding from? Well, I was a marginal member of my Catholic family, and I couldn't pursue a date within earshot of my parents, lest they say, "Enough, move out."

Steven answered the phone, I heard his frilly laugh for the first time, and asked him to dinner in Long Beach near where he lived. He didn't drive. I later found out he didn't have much of anything; he was deeply troubled, deeply needy. His deficiencies triggered into action every character flaw that I had had at the time. Although we were like oil and water, we started having sex quickly, then condomless (unprotected) sex because we both had said, "I love you." Of course, it wasn't a good reason for taking sexual risk, but in a moment of passion, in a moment of love, we took the risk.

Since he worked for Delta Airlines at the time, we were able to vacation in Florida. It was a nice enough time. I remember after going to do laundry coming back to our Disney World hotel room to find Steven wrapped in a towel, naked underneath, locked out of our hotel room!

He couldn't have looked more charming, nor sexier!

He was, it soon dawned on me, the most important commitment I'd ever undertaken. He had no family, his mom was a recovering heroine addict, his dad owned a bar in Long Beach that had this bumper sticker on the register: "If only I had pulled out, my life would be different."

The honeymoon was over almost before it got started. I caught Steven cheating. I found a condom wrapper under the bed, and a used condom in his laundry basket. He denied cheating, telling me that he examined himself for prostate cancer. He had already lied to me about being a survivor of cancer; he soon became the bane of my existence. And the more he denied it, the more furious I became. I should've obeyed my first instincts about him, but I stayed in the relationship, leaning on a stubborn sentiment that I could make things work. We fought and fought. I'd stay over at his apartment, affording me the opportunity to get away from my parents, to experience some independence.

Steven and I became co-dependent. In March 2003, I had a choice: my life with Steven or graduate school and my career, as I didn't have the psychic energy to do both. I was uncertain, anxious, and confused. Too fearful of the past, too preoccupied to see the present, I looked only to the future. Rather than dump Steven, I dumped grad school. I had to be with Steven all of the time; I loved him though, but it pains me to say, I didn't trust him. When I was away from him, I felt deprived of hearing his intoxicating words, "I love you." The fact that we were having sex without condoms I viewed as a loving gesture; we would be forever. Recalling all these feelings, I now see how tremendously naïve I was, but the impetus was indeed innocent: I wanted to be in love. And like so many people, I believed I was in love when I really wasn't. So it comes down to this: I needed Steven for touch, for sex, for validation, for a period of time, and I believe he needed me, but true love, clear now, wasn't a part of our relationship. I didn't know how to let him go.

I, consequently, found myself withdrawn from graduate school and working at Ruby Tuesday's in Oceanside, Long Island. Just seven months ago I had been on top of the world, commuting to and from Senator Hillary Clinton's Office, working at Lenox Hill Neighborhood House, making friends with fellow social work students. Apparently my relationship with Steven was known throughout Long Island's club scene. I was laughed at and pitied. I often called friends, to vent, to cry, to lament, to hope, and in my frenzied condition I lost weight, had irritable bowel syndrome and totally unraveled.

Once at Ruby Tuesday's the manager invited me to become part of the management team. I was doing exceedingly well. When once I left Ruby Tuesday's mid-shift, I had to see Steven because we had fought. I raced over to his nearby apartment; he wanted to have sex with me, and I let him. I thought having sex with him would be the answer to all our woes. When he couldn't orgasm, I started crying. Was I no longer attractive to him? Was he tired of me? I looked at him, trying to compose myself, to overcome my feelings of worthlessness.

I was exhausted. Exhausted from signing online and catching him in a gay chatroom with a new alias like piggybottom or sexinahurry23, weary from his feigned and untruthful attempts to reconcile with me after he had treated me like shit. I had also become tired of him; truth be told, I gradually realized that he had no interests, though sometimes he could be fun, dressing dress up in drag and singing songs by his favorite artist, Mariah Carey. One spring day, I cleaned myself up, psychologically steeled myself and went to work. Something about me must've clued in my colleagues, for they expressed concern about me, their looks saying, "You look unhappy, what's wrong?" I said nothing, for I couldn't find the words to describe how I felt. And if I could, I would likely have felt humiliated.

Somehow, fortuitously, Steven and I had our third break-up. I had felt so victimized by him, as if I'd been bullied and beaten, and I psychologically had been; true, no bruises to my body, but plenty to my psyche. Of course, at the time, I hadn't realized that I had been harmed psychologically, that I was a victim of cyclical violence, i.e., sexual violence. I wanted to love him so much that I allowed him to do with me what he wanted; I ignored my own needs and interests. Not a healthy situation to say the least. (Such a theme is all too common in gay films. Would a gay man's experience of life be different if the Roman Catholic Church, with her 1.2 billion members practiced the full incorporation of LGBTQ people into her communion?)

I promised never to go back to him. I was wounded, damaged. And my bank account was depleted, primarily because of Steven, as if I thought I could buy his love. I bought Steven a Burberry scarf, one that he loved, even a three-diamond ring from JC Penny. I had stopped going to Church, but studied Judaism because Steven was Jewish, thinking it would please him. When Steven showed up at my new job at Hofstra University, he brought some of the gifts I gave him with him, all mangled and destroyed.

I eventually had to face it, Steven was out of control; he made a scene at my work, and my new co-workers became alarmed. He shoved my coffee pot (already broken) and the Burberry scarf (already cut into a hundred pieces) into my hands. He'd already lost the diamond ring one drunken night at Penn Station. Said nasty things, like, "I hate you," then left in rage. My boss,

Tim Robey, who was an older gay man, (he had an Ed.D. from Columbia University), sensitively and compassionately cared for me. I needed human, gentle care. I'd forgotten that men could be gentle, and nothing moves me like gentleness. And then in a moment of paralyzing insight, I saw the horror of what Steven had done to me.

I filed a report with campus security, soon to be followed by Steven's worst voicemails ever. He threatened new acts of violence, just shy of saying, "I'll kill you." In one message he said, "I gave you AIDS." I was horrified! I broke out in a sweat, couldn't breathe, couldn't move. Was my life over? How long did I have? And then an inner voice, oily and gruesome said, "You got what you deserve. This is God's punishment for your having sex with men. And you will burn forever in hell." Maybe my mom was right! Maybe the Church was right!

I admit that every time I had sex without a condom, the thought of AIDS would ever so briefly loom in my mind. But when one is young, with a strong libido, one thinks one is invulnerable. Also, at that time, what options were there for gay men? Society told me that I couldn't get married, that risky, sexual behavior and drug use was "only normal" for gay men. So many gay movies had, and still have the same stereotypical plot line about failed and flailing gay relationships: two older teens or two men fall in love, they unravel (due to dysregulated behaviors, psychological turmoil or family troubles, likely rejection) seek redemption from or in a spurned lover, then reconcile to that love only to see the lover move on. I could look no where for affirmation of my sexual identity, that my life as a gay man could be healthy, happy and holy.

Straight people don't have death looming over their sex acts, it's not a consideration (though they too often practice unsafe sex). I chose not to play it safe. And I should've known better, but in the heat of the moment, I just wasn't careful.

And then to be told I had AIDS. I nearly lost it.

It isn't something anyone wants to hear, ever. I felt dead on the inside, catching the "gay disease," "Grid," "God's punishment for gay people"—I'd heard every unchristian comment made by a person of faith or no faith at all, I felt the tumult, the catastrophe of homophobia. I thought this is the reason why gay men cannot donate blood to blood banks like the American Red Cross, that our blood is always unwanted and denied, even if we prove we're HIV negative. But I do understand our reality: Gay men are an impulsive *fuck* away from a death sentence. And now I had likely caused my own death. I had hit rock bottom.

After I composed myself, I scheduled to get tested at a free health clinic (at Planned Parenthood in Hempstead, NY). I couldn't use my parent's health insurance lest they find out the results. Afterwards, I went to file a restraining order against Steven. I was stunned by how fair, balanced and compassionate, if not tender, the Nassau County cops were. They even joked with me, and made me feel better.

Like the character Nicodemus in the Gospel of John, I went to Jesus in the middle of the night, when I felt most desolate and alone. After looking at gay porn (it's strange, but it helped me to forget myself), I'd lay on my twin bed, and I'd think about my departure from social work school, my failed relationships with Jim and Steven. I'd think about my family and their lack of acceptance. I felt so alone and asked Jesus to help me. And a voice said, "You reach out to people, you want to help them, but you also need to help yourself," Jesus' message to me. And I embraced it.

His message made me reconsider my calling to become a priest. I wanted so much one day to celebrate Mass, to devote my life to prayer, to help homeless gays, kids lost in our huge cities. I had read about Jesuits like Matteo Ricci and Walter Ciszek who were committed to Jesus, and who served him in Asia, as missionaries to unknown and unchartered territories, one to a foreign mission, and the other to a Communist regime. I loved how these men spoke about mass, and how they dedicated their lives to the care of souls. I saw in them strong men, always hopeful, able to withstand distance from friends, and family, men whose lives were dedicated to the greater glory of God. I saw myself in them, and them in me.

I found myself back at www.nysj.org, back at reviewing everything Jesuit I could find. Of course, I felt unsettled by my past relationships, knowing how wounded I was. I sought out my pastor Fr. Gary Capadocia, and therapy with a clinical social worker, Rivka Kepler. I needed to be reintegrated, put back together again. I also felt, intuitively, that running back to discerning the priesthood might simply be an escape from a very negative period in my life. I promised, no matter what I thought, or did over the next months, that I wouldn't contact a vocation director until December. Six-months seemed a reasonable amount of time for a twenty three-year old to gain some added perspective on his life, and to become a more integrated young man. I fully understood Carl Jung's idea of individuation: to become a whole person, I needed to integrate myself, and include the archetypal shadow of ourselves that Jung says we would rather ignore.

In that time I returned to daily mass, to private prayer, to pious practices like praying before and with the Virgin Mary. I had more tattoos, inking the scapula on my arms, I thought what better way for a young, gay Catholic to ensure entrance into Heaven than by dying with the scapula inked on his body. They were my modern religious "medals."

I continued on in my studies in a Masters program in Humanities at Hofstra University and studied art, literature and Greek philosophy. I was introduced to writers like Henry Miller, Franz Kafka, and Kobo Abe. The American Trappist monk and theologian Thomas Merton once said that Henry Miller "is a kind of secular monk with a sexual mysticism." I felt closer to Miller than Merton; Miller encouraged people to have sex because it made them whole persons. Some believe the Church won't allow hetero-sexual priests to marry because if a priest had interocurse, then a family, he might lay claim on church property. Still, in each of them, I inferred their own self-understanding of themselves standing on the margins of society; thus, we were kindred spirits. By reading Miller and Kafka, I felt that I was a "Colossus" finding my way through the labyrinth of life; yet I desired to break free from my disenchantment with my life.

Through my faith, and through the inspiration of literature, I pieced together, stitch by stitch, my life. I also enjoyed working in the Office of Graduate Admissions. I went back out into the world, going to gay clubs, enjoying myself and some men, lamenting over failed hook-ups, once even shaving my entire body after a wasted experience with a man I brought back to my home while everyone was away. I felt something beyond guilt and self-loathing, I blushed with shame. I don't know, but I was learning: even bad experiences are "good" because they are part and parcel of the life experience. Heaven and hell is before us at all times.

With each month, I felt more and more alive, more joyful, even grateful. When I thought about the depth and breadth of a sacramental and priestly life in the Society of Jesus, I was filled with awe and longing. Thoughts about becoming a Jesuit moved from the back burner of my mind/soul to the front. I no longer felt it an impossibility to be one of them, a member of the Jesuit order. I had risked knowing myself in my new discernment, and I decided it was time to contact a vocation director; it was December 2003. I wrote Fr. Paul Arnold, S.J., the first Jesuit I would meet in person. My email to Fr. Paul came from my new *Gay Rights* inspired AOL Screen Name: UranianUrning71.

Uranian is the nineteenth century English adaptation of the German word *Urning*, which referred to an effeminate person of the third sex, per-haps a female with a male body. It was first mentioned by the German activist Karl Heinrich Ulrichs, whose *Research into the Riddle of Man-Male Love* preceded the use of the now recognized and accepted term, homosexual (the term gay wouldn't be universally used until the 1960s). Uranian was quickly picked up by Victorian Era social activists Edward Carpenter and John Addington Symonds, who spoke about a congenial love between men, a love for them that could bring about full democracy. "71" stood for 1871, the year Paragrah 175 (Section 175 in English) criminalized same-sex sex acts between men in Germany. Like this criminal code, the twentieth century St. Joseph Baltimore Catechism would also write about crimes against chastity, which in the same section, listed homosexuality, rape, fornication, lust, prostitution and masturbation. Nevertheless, most people who received an email from UranianUrning71@aol.com were puzzled, and they often asked, "What does your screen name mean?"

My email to Fr. Paul was brief; in it I stated generally who I was, but then added, "I am an integrated, young Catholic, gay man, who is now ready to honestly and freely respond to God's invitation to be a Jesuit priest." I continued, "I desire to learn how to obey God's call, and to manifest the courage to seriously commit to a period of discernment that may or may not lead to my entering the Society of Jesus." I ended by saying that "Since I was a young teenager, I both knew that I was gay, and that I was also hearing God's voice in prayer. I am not running away from who I am, I am a gay man, and cannot be a priest in the Diocese of Long Island because they will not accept homosexuals." Fr. Paul, replied, simply enough: "Let's meet."

Fr. Paul and I met at St. Ignatius Loyola Retreat House, in Manhasset. The first Jesuit Apostolate I would visit was the former home of the businessman and philanthropist Nicholas Brady and his wife Genevieve. As I walked up to the house, I noticed tiny, little faces, almost angelic, sticking out from the façade and brickwork. Later, I'd find out that Nicholas and Genevieve were childless, and that these faces possibly represented their good Roman Catholic desire to be fruitful and multiply, if not their languishment at their inability to conceive and fulfill the Church's moral standard for the ends of sacramental (heterosexual) marriage.

During that December meeting, Fr. Paul and I discussed the evolution of my vocation, and even my own coming out story. When I told him how my parents and family reacted to my sexuality, he looked sad, and suddenly withdrawn. Fr. Paul and I talked about the many gays in the Jesuit order. I told him that it didn't matter whether one was heterosexual or homosexual, I even added asexual to get a laugh; what mattered was the person's ability to be found by God, to love God's son, Jesus, and to do so with maturity, psychological integration, and the capacity to say "no," i.e. to be generous and generative in healthy ways. Fr. Paul gave me what would become a familiar, Charlie Brown-type look, and I couldn't tell if he was lost in the clouds, or lost in his thoughts about what he wanted to do with me.

Since first thinking about my vocation in 1995, I had matured, grew in self-confidence and became aware of who I was, and whose (God's) I was deeply within myself. As I prepared for greater familiarity with the Jesuits, God readied me and prepared me for future moments of graced consolation. Along the way, God gave me additional signs, which indicated the fulfilling way in which God's finger pointed at me while He said: *Be a Jesuit.* I prayed often the Anima Christi, a Catholic prayer attributed to St. Ignatius of Loyola:

> Soul of Christ, sanctify me.
> Body of Christ, save me.
> Blood of Christ, inebriate me.
> Water from the side of Christ, wash me.
> Passion of Christ, strengthen me.
> O Good Jesus, hear me.
> Within your wounds hide me.
> Permit me not to be separated from you.
> From the wicked foe, defend me.
> At the hour of my death, call me
> and bid me come to you
> That with your saints I may praise you
> For ever and ever. Amen.

I desired St. Ignatius' close relationship with Jesus, and I prayed that I could, while being a sexual celibate, joy in voluntary celibacy like him. It was through voluntary celibacy, or the vow of chastity, that God would intensify my availability to be with the people I served.

For two-and-a-half-years I grew to know Jesuit community life and vowed life in action; I went to every Jesuit Community in New York, meeting many less known Jesuits, even some outcasts. I asked every question I could, simple ones like, "What was it like celebrating your first mass?" and deeper ones like, "What's the most challenging part of being a priest in New York City?"

I met many Jesuits from New Jersey to Syracuse and beyond. I even met many future novices in a men's discernment group, which I formed in order to find and to give support to other men who believed they had nascent Jesuit vocations. There I met good friends like Jeff Plougher and Randy Costa, men whom God would take in different directions, but who would remain good friends. Jeff became a social worker as I would, while Randy is still a Jesuit.

In 2005, I started my application to the Jesuits after months of "dating" the Jesuits. I met with Brother Cale Dunlevy, a Regis High School grad. He was generous, caring, and did not whince when I self-identified as a gay man. Most Jesuits I met were gay. At the time, I couldn't tell if they were out or not, but I could certainly tell they were not going public with their sexuality. Internally I decried their unwillingness to come out publicly, and wondered why they didn't. I questioned the closet of the gay priesthood. I thought: it's not just LGBTQ youth that need saving, its older LGBTQ Catholics who have never heard about the mercy of God, people for whom the work of Walter Cardinal Kasper, the president Emeritus of the Pontifical Council for Promoting Christian Unity, was too many decades away from publication.

Brother Cale led me through a five-hour interview, which was as grueling in its length as it was in its scope of topics. I was asked everything from "Was I a bottom or a top?" to "Are you running from your sexuality?" to "Do you hate your alcoholic dad?" to "What do you do on Friday nights?" The "long interview" covered spirituality, religion, relationships, employment history, dreams, desires, and began a larger process to see whether or not I was a *good fit* for the Society of Jesus. It was as if the psychoanalyst D.W. Winnicott had applied his theories of object relations and the holding environment to the process of discernment that led the Provincial of any Jesuit Province to declare a man accepted, denied or deferred entrance to the Society of Jesus.

That spring, in 2005, I worked as the customer relations support person at the retail store Pottery Barn. I had already been District Employee of the month, and was being eyed for a management position. I liked the job well enough, and retreated to it after I quit my job at the St. Ignatius Loyola Retreat House. I fled a hostile working environment, where enmeshed professional relationships, splitting and triangulation allowed a berserk employee named Ana to practically run the place into the ground. Ana had cast some spell on the Jesuit director Fr. Jack Canale. While at Pottery Barn, I met Dana, the first transgendering (male to female) person I'd know, and with whom I'd dance with at a nearby "straight" bar during one of our colleague Janet's Pottery Barn night out. Then there was Kitty, a young, hot, curly-haired bombshell, whose children had no idea their mom went after hot Abercrombie and Fitch employees, boys whose bodies were hairless, whose vocabulary was small, but whose age was between eighteen and twenty five. One day, while in the stockroom Kitty, Dana and I got on the topic of breast implants. I naïvely said, "I never saw breast implants before." Kitty threw up her shirt and Victoria Secret bra and showed me her breasts! I hadn't seen breasts since having sex with my ex-girlfriend in high school. They saw my shock, my blush, and they laughed. I knew for sure I was accepted as a gay man. And I was proud to be accepted.

While I was being shown women's implants, dancing with trans people, and interviewing for the Society of Jesus, the health of Pope John Paul II further declined. I lamented his suffering, and wept at his death. The election of a new pope intrigued me, its process labyrinthine, secretive and medieval like, yet a process filled with so much hope. So many wondered aloud: Who will the next Pope be?, Will he call Vatican III?, What will the new Pope decide about divorce or married clergy or birth control or homosexuality?

These issues mattered to me or rather the priestly me I was becoming. When Pope Emeritus Benedict XVI was elected, my reaction was visceral, though Jesuitical. So many Jesuits I had met told me about their reaction to "God's Rottweiler." One Jesuit even apologized to a class of African-American students at Harlem's Jesuit run Cristo Rey School. He had screeched, "Oh, Fucking Shit!"

About this time, I learned of my admission to the Society of Jesus. I was also finishing up a year of coursework at CUNY-Hunter College; my safety plan included completing my social work degree as well as earning a a masters degree in performance studies from New York University. To finish my social work degree, I wanted to work with the notable gay social worker Gabe Malloy. I was enrolled in his class; he knew about my discernment and looked out for me, meeting with me from time to time. I sensed that he felt unsure about my choice, wondering, as he did for all the LGBTQ youth he wrote about in his seminal texts, whether or not I was going to flourish, fester, or fall apart.

Malloy invited me to edit an essay I wrote on queer pedagogy, a work that my future Novice Master John Languish would ask me not to publish before I formally entered the Jesuits. Fr. Languish told me, in so many words, that you will not be advanceable in the Society of Jesus if that work is published. Fr. Languish's voice didn't welcome challenge or another opinion. His voice did ask me about another publication I had published in the Harvard Gay and Lesbian Review Worldwide. Fr. Languish neither praised nor condemned my publication, he was just silent; I wondered: Will he be a silent, male figure in my life?, yet another man unable to experience, express, or disclose his inner life?

Despite all this shortcoming, I felt that my heart was on fire with the love of God. I was eager to begin my religious life. It had been many years since my high-school self first heard God's invitation to "Come and See" or "to be a Fisher of Men." In my vocation story, there was no burning bush, no resurrected dry bones, no talking snakes, no eschatological/apocalyptic visions as in the Book of Revelation, just a simple calling, the real meaning of *vocare*—to call.

My Spiritual Autobiography told stories about the still, small voice that followed me everywhere and reflected my desire to be a young, gay Catholic priest. I felt confirmed, consoled, called, and remained full of gratitude. I often returned to a prayer by the former Jesuit Superior General, Fr. Pedro Arrupe, which was quickly becoming my favorite poem. Arrupe writes:

Nothing is more practical than
finding God, than
falling in Love
in a quite absolute, final way.
What you are in love with,
what seizes your imagination, will affect everything.
It will decide
what will get you out of bed in the morning,
what you do with your evenings,
how you spend your weekends,
what you read, whom you know,
what breaks your heart,
and what amazes you with joy and gratitude.
Fall in Love, stay in love,
and it will decide everything.

That summer my family threw me a surprise going-away-party at my brother's house in Massapequa. Friends from college, high school, family members, including cousins I hadn't seen since my grandmother Katherine's funeral, were there. Drinks, food and cheer abounded. I was happy, and it was gorgeous out. Then something hit me, I looked around and as I did, I realized I was looking for Samuel Beckett. But he wasn't present. I knew my family had intentionally not invited him. To them my entrance into the Jesuits symbolized a victory over my sexuality.

I was the only gay person present at my party, and I felt lonely. My family believed that they were celebrating the *death* of my being gay in as much as they celebrated my great commission, to go make disciples of all the Earth.

At the end of the summer, my parents moved to Riverhead, to avoid the impending "Blackening" of Valley Stream, as much as they desired a new home. I laughed on the inside when some of my parent's new neighbors were African-American. During the drives between Valley Stream and Riverhead, I thought about my own coming move, to St. Andrew Hall, the Jesuit Novitiate, located in Syracuse, New York. As I drove the Long Island Expressway, with my Labrador Zoe breathing heavily from the backseat, I slipped on the soundtrack from the Showtime original series *Queer as Folk*. I cried hard when Heather Small's *Proud* came on; I sang along, "What did I do today to make myself feel proud?"

I was proud to have heeded God's call by entering the Society of Jesus.

Chapter 6

The Novice Master's Plantation

In our society, which we wish to be called by the name Jesus, let whoever desires to fight under the sacred banner of the Cross, and to serve only God and the Roman pontiff, His vicar on earth, after a solemn vow of perpetual chastity,-let him keep in mind that he is part of a society, instituted for the purpose of perfecting souls in life and in Christian doctrine, for the propagation of the faith through public preaching, ministering the word of God, spiritual macerations, works of charity, and especially through the teaching of the young and uninstructed in the Christian precepts; and lastly for giving consolation to believers in hearing their confessions. Let him think first of God, then of the rule of this order, which is the way to Him; and let him follow after the end proposed by God with all his strength.

—The Formula for the Society of Jesus, as presented to Pope Paul III, who approved the new Order with the Apostolic Letter "Regimini militantis Ecclesiae" on September 27, 1540.

When a Jesuit leaves the Society of Jesus, his brothers often refer to him as "dead to us" (although this is not written anywhere this expression is very much a part of Jesuit life). They coolly stop communication with him, and often, unless they are good friends, cease being in relationship with him. That's the reason why I was surprised, some months after my departure from the Jesuits, to find an email from Fr. Peter Cooper, the Jesuit priest who worked in Washington, D.C.

In the email, Fr. Peter told me that my religious superiors were *timid*, that they should have supported me more, that he wanted to pray with me, for my return to the Society someday, for my becoming an openly gay ordained priest. What struck me most about Fr. Peter's email wasn't his hope that I'd respond to God's invitation to become a priest, or that he knew about a "gay-affirming" Catholic documentary titled *Owning Our Faith* that was circulating through "gay friendly" urban parishes, but that he called my religious superiors "timid." According to the Merriam-Webster dictionary timid means: 1) lacking in courage or self-confidence, *e g*, a *timid* person or 2) lacking in boldness or determination, *e.g.*, a timid policy.

Fr. Peter was on the mark: my superiors were indeed timid. My first superior was Fr. John Languish, a Maryland Province Jesuit who was an anointed one, or golden boy—as such; he was sent to the Novitiate to become Novice Master. Where, presumably, he'd serve another term in formation, a right of passage for any Jesuit who had designs on becoming Provincial or superior of men in his jurisdiction.

Fr. John Languish reminded me of Dilbert from the Scott Adams cartoon. When we met, he was almost fifty, with sky blue eyes, a Kangaroo pouch for a stomach. He was the first person I met that loved Lady Gray tea, and whose shirts were sharply pressed, while his shirt cuffs were always turned inward. In his bedroom hung an obscure painting of the lost sheep. I could never tell how he saw himself as a shepherd; whereas, he had been superior of scholastics (Jesuits in the First Studies program), served as Socius or Assistant Provincial; in short he was always in charge, and had been rarely, if ever, missioned as a subordinate. Fr. John never got dirty with the poor, he surely never carried a sheep on his neck. To be the "Good Shepherd" of the Gospel of John, he'd have to get his hands dirty—again this would never happen.

From the day I moved in to St. Andrew's Hall, the Jesuit Novitiate, in Syracuse, New York, Fr. John Languish was in charge, determined to submit novices, "who could tell him nothing about the Society of Jesus" to the test of discernment. To Fr. John: the Novitiate was a time of testing, to "leave one way or another", like a Jesuit Scholastic (priest candidate) who professed First Vows through this Jesuit Vow Formula:

> Almighty and eternal God, I, (insert man's name), understand how unworthy I am in Your divine sight. Yet I am strengthened by Your infinite compassion and mercy, and I am moved by the desire to serve You.
>
> I vow to Your divine majesty, before the most holy Virgin Mary and the entire heavenly court, perpetual poverty, chastity

and obedience in the Society of Jesus. I promise that I will enter
into this same Society to spend my life in it forever.

I understand these things according to the Constitutions of
the Society of Jesus.

Therefore, by Your boundless goodness and mercy and
through the blood of Jesus Christ, I humbly ask that you judge
this total commitment of myself acceptable; and as you have
freely given me the desire to make this offering, so also may You
give me the abundant grace to fulfill it.

Or as a Jesuit Novice who left the Novitiate and returned
to life as a layperson, either to marry, and "be fruitful and multiply," or to live life as a celibate gay man, the only *authentic*
alternative for a man who, to Fr. John, was oriented to same-sex
sexual relationships.

On the Novice Master's Plantation, a term we novices used to refer
to our tenure of servitude under the care of Fr. John, there was one quietly
spoken rule: *keep Fr. John happy.* For many of us that meant submitting to
Fr. John's worldview, to day-by-day, becoming more Jesuitical while neglect-
ing our true selves. For some, the process of Jesuit-reprogramming, or Jesuit
Boot Camp was positive, a process they desired to submit to as a means to
an end, professing First Vows as a Brother or Scholastic.

From the moment I arrived on the Novice Master's Plantation, I
yearned to be my truest, most authentic self. I desired a spirituality of integration, as espoused by the former Jesuit Wilkie Au, who wrote a text I'd
turn to time and again, *By Way of the Heart* or another text he wrote with
his wife Noreen Canon Au *The Discerning Heart.* They like me cherished
St. Iranaeus, who said, that: "The glory of God is the human person fully
alive." Wilkie Au, like the Jesuit historian Fr. Hugo Rahner, S.J., believed,
"A healthy spirituality cannot be built on the ruins of the human person";
he continues, "A healthy spiritual life respects human wholeness and does
not pit it in opposition to holiness and religious commitment. Only such a
holistic approach can successfully inculcate the habits of the heart that have
made the religious path a genuine way to holiness and growth of the total
person." These quotes were like mantras to me.

Before we considered ourselves a community, we shared our vocation
stories. It was the first time we'd hear each other's pilgrim-journey to St.
Andrew Hall. The men in the second year were nicknamed by a surly, preco-
cious guy, named Mello who played guitar and wrote folk music. To many of
the novices, he was a hero; to Fr. John Languish, he was an anti-hero, whose
days were numbered; I heard him sing a sexist song that chided women, and
speak about male chauvinism during a "Come and See Jesuit-life" weekend

in 2004. His nicknames for my *Secundi* (the Latin term for second, or men in the second year of the Novitiate) spoke volumes about the men I was with, but they were in many ways cruel.

"Z-Dicks" was a redheaded, fat, guy from Buffalo. He arrived because his principal, then Socius, and he were good friends. From the moment I met him he was often drunk or angry; he spoke to few, and when he did, it was a barrage of unprocessed grievances. He was miserable. "Jolly" was a Jesuit-high school alum, who attended an Ivy League school; he made noises, like a kid, always laughed at one thing or another, perhaps to cope with his self-alienation and maltreatment by Z-Dicks. "Tyler-no-plain-clothes" was a crooning, Neil Diamond loving kid from outside Boston; he was very attractive (all my gay and straight friends lusted after him); wearing only khakis and collared shirts, he railed against liberalism, and I was sorry to hear him say that he'd never fallen in love. Even when he cleaned, "Tyler-no-plain clothes" often wore pleated pants. "The Bishop" was a hefty gay who had lost his dad and a brother; he prided himself on being far above the rest, and never criticized the Society; it was always hard to converse with him because one was always "not good enough." "The Professor" was some kind of engineer, the only brother candidate in my two years; he hardly spoke, always cooked with crock pots, and forced his understanding of poverty on the rest of us. "The Dolphin" was a Le Moyne college alum, who was also my Angel; he told me to bring sunglasses to Syracuse, that's all he said I'd need. He was nicknamed "the Dolphin" because he spent his free time in the pool, swimming outdoors or indoors depending on the season. "Paddy O'Toolihan" was an Irish guy, who went to a state school in New Jersey, reserved, inexperienced, but all together a lovely guy. "India" was a half-Indian, white-privileged, elite, who majored in history and whose love for India led him to cook Indian food, speak about Indian culture, rail against Pakistan and win a prestigious Truman Scholarship to study abroad while attending a Jesuit college. "Doctor" was a Ph.D. gentleman who drank Rob Roys with Fr. John Languish; he worked in higher education administration, and was often found at the bar with "Z-Dicks." Rick rounded out the bunch; he had no nickname, and came from Long Island. His parents were shocked when he entered religious life, hoping he'd become a doctor, an orthodontist or a lawyer. Mello never gave Rick a nickname, perhaps because Rick had no pretense, or ego, who spoke the truth as it was, and who often received the private ire of Fr. John Languish.

There were four of us in my class, after a fifth re-accepted man hadn't shown up to the Novitiate. We were called *Primi* (or first, and represented the first year men). There were two from the New England Province, one from Maryland and me from New York. In times past some sixty men plus might enter the Novitiate and populate places like Hyde Park's St. Andrew-on-the-Hudson. In 2005 there were four men who represented the hopes and dreams of Jesuits from Maine to South Carolina, and mission territories like Jamaica and Micronesia. Mello didn't nickname us, though Z-Dicks did try, especially when drunk.

In my class there was Chris, a Xaverian High School alum, who sipped rum and cokes in the library and played strategy games on the Internet until he left after the thirty-day Long Retreat. There was Matthew and Kris whom I grew to call respectively Tweedledee and Tweedledum. Matthew was an older gentleman, some forty-years plus at entrance, who had a history of changing jobs, and as far as I know, his only assignment in the Society of Jesus was completing his dissertation. He had started his dissertation before he entered; some eleven years later, it may remain unfinished, such is likely the case because Tweedledee always used multiple colored pens to outline thoughts, which he kept private, unless he was slaving over his favorite meal "sweaty meats." Tweedledee once told me that women who wear fish net stockings like to dominate men during sex. When he was fast tracked for the priesthood, I knew that once a homophobic man is approved for ordination there is no turning back.

Kris, or Tweedledum, had a woeful gait, year after year gravity had helped him slouch more; he had earned a job with the Peace Corps, priding himself at drinking Budweiser or Pabst Blue Ribbon at dive bars from Massachusetts, to New York to Romania. Kris was never happy, not even at seeing me leave the Jesuits. One Jesuit publication commented that, Kris "has a way about him that reminds you of a priest from an old movie. He's Pat O'Brien in *Angels with Dirty Faces,* Bing Crosby in *The Bells of St. Mary's,* or Karl Malden in *On the Waterfront*—the kind of priest who might teach you how to throw a left hook." To me Matt and Kris were more like the characters from Lewis Carroll's *Through the Looking-Glass,* and *What Alice Found There*; they dressed alike, their thoughts undifferentiated, and they suffered from separation anxiety when one of them tried to individuate. I often thought: are they one, or cyborgs, whose mind and matter were bridged? They also reminded me of the lyrics from the poet John Byrom, whose epigram goes,

> Some say, compar'd to Bononcini
> That Mynheer Handel's but a Ninny
> Others aver, that he to Handel
> Is scarcely fit to hold a Candle
> Strange all this Difference should be
> 'Twixt Tweedle-dum and Tweedle-dee!

To round out the men who made up the Novitiate in 2005–2006 were two assistant staff members, Fr. Jack Finnish and Fr. Jerry Conscience. Fr. Jack Finnish was the autoharp, piano playing, whimsical, artist-in-residence, who often received Fr. John Languish's "Eyebrow" when he was in conference. Fr. Jack often challenged Tweedledee and Tweedledum, but Fr. John wouldn't have it; it was the Novice Master's Plantation. Fr. Jerry Conscience was snarky, loving, compassionate; he and I bonded and became friends. If it weren't for Fr. Jerry, I would have left the Jesuits in June 2006. To me, Fr. Jerry is a saint. Cecilia Merry was the Novice Master's assistant. She had degrees in philosophy and library science, and a family—the only woman some of the novices would talk too; still some of them wouldn't go near her but to thank her. She was generous and shy, and Fr. John Languish often remarked about her meekness, a remark that I don't think would've pleased her. But, of course, meekness is one of the "virtues" the Jesuits try to inculcate in all of us; thus, we do what we're told.

Those were the men and one woman with whom I prayed, lived, studied, and recreated at St. Andrew Hall, a Novitiate that included three one-family houses named after the Jesuit boys saints and patron saints of Novices, Aloysius Gonzaga, Stanislaus Kostka, and John Berchmans.

Shakespeare himself could not have created such a motley, intriguing, surprising group of people to strut their stuff upon the stage of St. Andrew Hall.

Back in the chapel those first few days of the Novitiate, Fr. John Languish expected us to share our vocation story. It would be an activity through which community would be formed, and through which we'd come to know one another as Jesuit novices. The two-page instructions, printed on goldenrod paper, gave controlled and measured prayer points. I remember nothing in those instructions about going to see Fr. John if we had questions about how to tell our story. Why would we? It was our personal narrative, a mini spiritual autobiography, one that emphasized (orally) key moments in our lives when God was close to us, or when God was far from us, key moments that confirmed and affirmed our callings, our Baptismal invitations to serve Jesus Christ.

During the pre-conference, Fr. John never cautioned us to leave out details, or not to speak casually or from the heart. Fr. John never said, "do not cry" or "be emotional."

Once our stories commenced, men spoke about proximity to Jesus, about being born again, about the death of family members, the absence of family members; they spoke about loveless straight relationships, when older men in their thirties and forties didn't speak about relationships, I looked at them, and I sensed, through my "gaydar" that they were gay, like me.

Why weren't they speaking about their sexuality? The straight men spoke freely about carnal relationships with women. Some men looked up from time to time, others at Fr. John Languish for affirmation that vocation telling was going according "to his plan." Others looked at the reflections on the walls, the hued colors from the stain glass windows. Stained glass windows that told the story of the North American Jesuit Martyrs, men like Isaac Jogues and John Brebeuf, who were killed by Native Americans and for whom the movie Black Robe tells an anecdotal story of their martyrdom. But about the windows of their minds, their souls, were they to be kept closed forever?

As my turn neared, I felt such a pit in my stomach. Not one gay novice or staff member had revealed their sexuality. I thought about Jesus' loving me as a gay man, I thought about Fr. Paul Arnold's and my many meetings, where he said "do not deny yourself," or my meetings with the vocation director Brother Cale Dunlevy, who walked me through the application process and told me "I'm proud of you, that your not running away from your sexuality." I thought about Fr. Jorge Cid, my Provincial, and the acceptance letter he wrote me, welcoming me to the Society of Jesus, thanking me for my generosity and for the person God was forming me to be. I thought about my conversations with Fr. Jerry Mettlesome, who told me "The Society welcomes you" and "Don't be afraid, with us, you will become a great, chaste, gay, priest." Following my departure, Fr. Jerry became a Judas to me, still we both practiced our vow of obedience deeply and honestly.

As I started to reflect on my vocation, I went through the standard speak. I spoke about Christian service, e.g., being a Eucharistic minister. I spoke about my Christian family, e.g., how my family identified as Catholic and not German. I spoke about being confronted by a woman who told me any Catholic who works with Senator Hillary Cllinton is going to hell because "Clinton supports abortion."

I spoke about the movements in my soul that led me away from my entering the Diocese of Rockville Center or the Marist Fathers. I spoke about being wined and dined by Long Island's "Mansion Murphy." Or about how the Marist Fathers accepted me after I penned, literally, my spiritual autobiography on one summer's visit to Boston. I spoke about my love for the Franciscans, their poverty, their closeness to the poor. I spoke about St. Anthony of Padua and St. Francis of Assisi; about the Jesuits I met, Fathers Matteo Ricci and Walter Ciszek. I laughed, saying I was the quintessential online Jesuit vocation, that I was trending; I was the #JesuitVocation before Twitter even existed. I spoke about why I didn't match well with the Franciscans or Dominicans, whose American provinces were "divided" along liberal and conservative lines; this was code for gay-friendly or gay-hating provinces.

Once the superficial formalities were out, I looked around the room and acknowledged an even split between gay and straight novices. Yet, in hours of telling stories, not one gay person identified himself as gay. I closed my eyes, and then opened them to look over to the wall, beyond the altar, to a rainbow of color shining on the wall. I disappeared into those colors, a disappearance of ego as happens in a mystical experience. And when I came back to myself, words came to me, "I am with you, and I love you." And then, "Do not be afraid." Little did I know that I had stopped speaking. My eyes welled with tears. Tyler-no-plain-clothes moved as if to come to me, but remained seated.

I then spoke about my coming out, the months when my Catholic mom didn't speak to me her son, how hurt I was. I spoke about how thankful I was that my vocation was nurtured, that I as a gay, Catholic man, could respond to God's invitation to be a priest. That I, like my straight peers, could pursue life in Jesus, in a company of men founded by the Basque Nobleman, St. Ignatius of Loyola.

When I looked from the wall to those around me, I was surprised. I had always been a shy kid who disliked public speaking. And I had now revealed my most inner self to all these men. I felt that I had done the right thing, that I had been faithful to my True Self. I was then flooded with joy, and with gratitude, for I felt I had not only represented myself but the many LGBTQ youth for whom I was hoping to help experience the fullness of human flourishing in their faith community.

After the final vocation stories were shared, we had mass, each receiving the Eucharist. We had sanctified our personal narratives by taking, breaking, sharing and eating the body and blood of Jesus Christ; however, once we left that chapel, Tweedledee and Tweedledum never spoke to me again. While we had "related" to each other before that day, the only conversation we had after that was cursory. Their silence disturbed me, it "Othered" me. They'd pass me in the hallway and look the other way, never again inviting me to join them for a drink—for anything.

My *Secundi*'s range of interaction with me was in keeping with the spectrum of their personalities and phobias, *e.g.*, internalized homophobia, homophobia or gynophobia. Thankfully there were more of them for me to interact with, which made for a great relief after every first year novice conference ended.

Fr. John Languish used the anteceding days to orient us to the Novitiate, to the schedule (the *Ordo*). He informed us about our monthly stipend, $60 for first year men, $75 for second year men. From the assistant novice masters, we learned about our schedule of cooking, cleaning and ministry. Fr. John assigned us our spiritual directors. Fr. John and I were matched. I'd meet with him weekly that first year, like any other first year novice. The flow of the Novitiate was growing in an optimal way, and Fr. John was happy, day-by-day, while Tweedledee, Tweedledum, and Z-Dicks treated me like shit. By the way, Fr. John never said anything about my vocation story. But he would!

Still that first year I made good friends. I cooked Saturday meals with India, Jolly and Tyler-no-plain-clothes. The Dolphin, Rick, and I traveled to Cazenovia, NY, and since we were the Long Island Boys, we stuck together. In Cazenovia we spent weekly break days at a many roomed villa house owned by the LeMoyne College Jesuit Community, one overlooking the serene but sulfer smelling lake. We bonded over the Roosevelt Field Mall, Snapple and beaches. We bonded over the Novice Master's idiosyncrasies; for instance, Fr. Languish always threatened his novices with pomposities like, "Permit me to tell you," "To be clear," "Now, brother," "Courage," "Get what you need Brother," or my personal favorite, "Let me tell you how and in what way." We all knew Fr. John was being passive aggressive when he said, "No worries." To Fr. John we were in the Novitiate on God's time, to discern nothing more than whether or not we were called to be Jesuits. To Fr. John that time might be borrowed, whereas men like Mello quickly were dismissed, and others like Rick, sought dismissal on their own (freely).

During Thanksgiving weekend, alums of the Novitiate are invited back to join in the celebration—a raucous environment, with top shelf alcohol, a first-class feast, whose dinner might start at 5pm and end at 2 am. Those nights were long, where you had to drink or eat until the Novice Master gave some sign that you were *free* to go. While one might be tired from hearing the same "Fr. John as the hero" or "Fr. John saved the day" story, leaving too early would be noted by the raising of his eyebrow. That Thanksgiving another anointed one or golden boy returned to the Novitiate—Fr. John's first beadle, the novice who directs the other novices to clean, who in turn is a conduit through which the Novice Master's happiness, discomfort or ire is relayed in common speak. Mr. Philip Fine was Fr. John's Anointed One, his Beloved, though many of us could see Philip's need of Fr. John for the purpose of ascending the Jesuit corporate ladder.

Philip read from the beadle logbook, one that records journal entries about novice "funny moments," serving to capture the lighter moments of these first two-years of Jesuit formation. As Philip read the stories to us, we heard about the time the Dolphin accosted an employee in Mexico while ordering Starbucks; he was suffering from caffeine withdrawal. Philip told us about the time Tyler-no-plain-clothes replicated a favorite blueberry pie. He used a favorite recipe inspired by the Jesuits on a Native American reservation he worked at with the Bishop. Somehow the wrong ingredients were tripled, sugar was left out; the pies were bland and the consistency was of paste. The stories were funny enough; thankfully, Philip took Fr. John out for some drinks, which meant after clean up using the unfortunately nicknamed "John Paul II" dishwasher, the JP II, we could retire or watch television.

That night many of us packed into a room to watch baseball. There were many fans, while others played pinochle, risk or walked in threes, still the "running theory" was that two-by-two walks might lead to secret same-sex intimacy between novices! That night Philip drove Fr. John's Toyota Solara, black, with leather interior and a sun roof, a two-door coupe that Fr. John said "came with the job." Fr. John was not a Franciscan, his understanding of poverty was skewed. Well, in truth, a car came with the job, but the goal for Fr. John was to stay happy, especially since he had such overt designs on becoming provincial. He could've driven a Honda Civic, or like us a Toyota Camry; in truth, we had too many cars, seven cars for the novices and one each for every staff member. By entering the Jesuits, I had stepped up at least two rungs on the class ladder. I went from middle class to upper, intellectual middle class. Though we had no income, we had communities and villas across the United States, and in notable American vacation spots like London, Paris, Barcelona, Vienna and Rome.

That night Philip returned with Fr. John, coming into the television room, where some of us were watching the baseball game. They were clearly spirited, smelling of drink. The Novice Master loved his Rob Roy. As they stood there, I started to feel a hand on the back of my head; I didn't panic, because it was gentle, soft, caressing, loving. As it drifted lower, it stayed a little too long for my comfort. I looked over and up, seeing my Novice Master's watery eyes. I couldn't infer what he was telling me; he so often had to be reserved, controlled, measured. His look frightened me, his touch confused me. Fr. John was the Novice Master, a man with so much power and authority. I never spoke to anyone about it, for who would believe me?—I wasn't publicly one of his favorites. I so desired to be a Jesuit, and soon I'd be heading to the Gonzaga Eastern Point Retreat House where I'd make the thirty-day Long Retreat and finally, where I'd make an Election, the Ignatian Spirituality term for decision making, to enter and continue my formation with the Jesuits. I couldn't risk asking Fr. John what his touch meant, lest he think I'd be accusing him of something improper. But I wanted to know: Why did you touch me? Loneliness? A need for touch? Love? Again, Fr. John had never disclosed much to us novices, never revealing anything personal.

My "gaydar" is usually pretty accurate, as I was almost certain that he was a gay man, one likely conflicted about his sexuality. Still I wondered: Is the Catholic Church telling me that priesthood and sexuality, being generatively gay or straight, are mutually exclusive? Isn't that just what got the Church into scandal in the first place?

Soon I'd write my Provincial,

> While in the Novitiate I have often prayed for the grace *to be who I am becoming*. Whether it is in community life, refugee re-settlement, studying the Society's documents and Spanish, or as an educator, home gutter and cancer-care technician, the vows of poverty, chastity and obedience have enabled me to serve [my neighbors] with freedom, compassion and generosity. My continued desire for humility, charity and gratitude witnesses a profound sense of love for religious life in the Society of Jesus. My own Novitiate experience has confirmed what my prayer tells me: that living the vows in community, as a Jesuit, is the place where God is calling me to live out my own principle and foundation. Clearly, the preparation for vowed life in the real world as a Jesuit has been extraordinary!
>
> By professing perpetual vows of poverty, chastity and obedience, I act out of complete and perfect love, finding the initiative in grace and nature, to courageously choose a Jesuit life *always ready for more*.

In that letter, I didn't mention my sexuality. I had been reprocessed; surviving novice life on the Novice Master's Plantation meant that I had to suffer from remaining in an unpleasant situation. As I re-read James Alison's *Faith Beyond Resentment*, I realized how true it is that you have to be yourself, also confirmed by Thomas Merton's concept of the true self. I was also influenced by the Jesuit priest James Empereur's *Spiritual Direction and the Gay Person*: I longed to be the authentic self he says God created me to be. During that fall, older Jesuits who were in charge of my care, came out to me during late night encounters in kitchens or darks spaces. Some of these hugs made me feel uncomfortable. I had hoped that I wasn't being used or misled by the gay Jesuits I met in in Jesuit communities along the East Coast. But I always listened, I always encouraged, and I hoped the same in return.

That winter, my first Christmas in Jesuit life, I returned home. After dinner with my parents at their newly established home in Riverhead, I drove to the movie theatre, where I watched Ang Lee's *Brokeback Mountain*. I saw the film alone, because my parent's move put me an hour's drive from my nearest friends. Like the film's character, Ennis, I felt desperately am-biguous about my new life. While I might have longed for a lover like Ennis' Jack, I led a reasonably happy life as a Jesuit novice. In fact, I had stopped using gay porn, and felt alive without it. Chastity wasn't so bad, and in my case it was required.

With the smell of popcorn still on me, I drove the darkened Long Island Expressway back to Riverhead. I'd been reading the gay poet C.P. Cavafy, some of his verses still lingering in my mind while I drove, I saw myself, my pursuit of love and sex in the young men he wrote about, but in reality his young manhood.

I was soon preparing myself for thirty-plus days of silence, at the Gónzaga Eastern Point Jesuit Retreat House, in Gloucester, Massachusetts. The thirty-day Long Retreat is the time in one's Jesuit life when he is the most monastic. In silence Jesus and I would become one, and this was the time when my invitation to be a Jesuit priest was confirmed and affirmed. As Fr. John Languish would soon tell me, and often, "Courage, to be continued"; however, I refused to be a sexual closet case, including the clerical closet. There would be many hurdles I know, not the least of which were my two remaining classmates, but I was determined to be myself.

Chapter 7

On the Road with Tweedledee and Tweedledum

St. Ignatius of Loyola takes retreatants through a four-week system of exercises that entail meditations, contemplations, examinations, reflections, and prayer periods, all in an effort to help persons articulate St. Ignatius' vision for them, as stated in *Spiritual Exercise 23*:

> The human person is created to praise, reverence, and serve God our Lord and by this means to save their soul. And the other things on the face of the earth are created for the human person and that they may help them in prosecuting the end for which they are created. From this it follows that the human person is to use them as much as they help them on to their end, and ought to rid themselves of them so far as they hinder them from doing it.

From January to February 2006, I entered a deep silence, praying for five hours a day for God to find me, and that in His finding me, that He would confirm my desire to be a Jesuit priest. As a pastime, I fed the mute swans, two parents and two babies, whose strength and courage would become a metaphor for the relationship that I wanted to pursue with God. They were such graceful, beautiful animals. I thought about William Butler Yates' poem titled, *The Wild Swans at Coole,*

> Unwearied still, lover by lover,
> They paddled in the cold
> Companionable streams or climb the air;

Their hearts have not grown old;
Passion or conquest, wander where they will,
Attend upon them still.
But now they drift on the still water,
Mysterious, beautiful;
Among what rushes will they build,
By what lakes' edge or pool
Delight men's eyes when I awake some day
To find they have flown away?

Fr. John Languish encouraged us to journal, suggesting that the journals we wrote would be crucial to conferences on the Vows, Ignatian Spirituality and Jesuit life for our second year of the Novitiate, but that they might also become an important part of our second thirty-day retreat, some fifteen to twenty-five years from now, when we would, if asked by the Society of Jesus, profess Final Vows and become fully incorporated members of the Jesuits, more commonly referred to as "men with the Fourth Vow."

In my journal from the retreat, I prayed with Annotations 266 and 268 on January 16th, 2006. I asked for the grace "to know Christ more intimately, to love Christ more intensely and to follow Christ more closely." I meditated on the Jesus of history, who is faith proclaimed on earth, and I longed to consecrate myself to Him. I asked myself, What do the characters of the Gospels see in the youthful Christ? My reflection for January 26th included these comments, "Jesus spoke about love, he spoke about duty to God, he spoke about the Kingdom and I—I could do nothing but savor and listen and be ever more attracted to imitate him. I could simply be in his presence, be willing to find a hope in him that replaced my doubt with joy, all my fear with peace."

As the retreat came to an end, I wrote about my anxieties of hitting the road with Matt and Kris, and lamented Chris' departure. I wrote, "I already feel the effects of Chris' leaving the group. I already feel a sense of uncertainty with Kris and Matt. I can only hope that the Lord provides me with what I need: namely, the grace of a new introduction to Matt and Kris. We are the only three Novices, representing three Provinces. I don't expect either of them to become my best friend, but it would be nice to always be included."

Even in those thirty-days of silence Fr. John Languish failed to confront their homophobia. He permitted them to continue even after Kris had played Keno and won $500.00 during a "retreat break day," that is a day when St. Ignatius offers the retreatants an opportunity to rest and relax.

Kris and Matt turned the day into a drink-fest. We went to the Crow's Inn, the site of the dive bar in the movie *The Perfect Storm*. Then to a second, less visible dive bar, where Kris told stories about Romania, then quietly won on Keno. When Fr. John Languish found out about Kris' superciliousness and insolent behavior, he confronted him, all of us, and quite unreasonably, Chris, because by then, it was clear that Fr. John did not believe Chris had a Jesuit vocation.

When it was my turn to meet with Fr. John, I wept, because all I wanted was to fit in, to be liked by these two men who were "my classmates, my sixth Novitiate experiment, an added cross to bear." Fr. John couldn't care less about Kris' playing Keno; he was absurdly indignant with Chris' ordering a $75.00 bottle of French Champagne. It was Kris who invited the other Chris to order anything on the menu at the local SoHo themed restaurant. Of course Fr. John did not end the retreat; we assuaged his ire when we promised to be "good boys." Mostly; he knew that our leaving would be a huge embarrassment for him, that it might even affect his chances to become Provincial.

By then I knew, Fr. John just wanted "good novices" who'd help him ascend the ranks. After all, St. Ignatius' order was styled on militaristic language. It was also the age of the Jesuits' Strategic Discernment, and the United States Assistancy was already planning on downsizing territories and province leadership, which meant, that, ten years from my entrance the U.S. Jesuits would have five provinces, and many hundreds of fewer men.

Before I left the retreat house, Fr. Len Marigold, a Pink Floyd fan, a scholar of the Jesuit poet Gerard Manley Hopkins, a graduate from the John Hopkins University, blessed my miraculous medal. I implored the Virgin Mary to come to my aid as I went on the road with Tweedledee and Tweedledum. While Fr. John Languish thought we were modeling St. Ignatius' pilgrim journey, to me, I was entering either on Joseph Conrad's *Heart of Darkness* or embarking on Jack Kerouac's *On the Road*! In that last journal entry from the diary of my Long Retreat, I wrote too optimistically that being with Matt and Kris will be about "sharing our experiences with one another, sharing our knowing and relating to Christ, as friends, brothers." But quickly, Matt and Kris turned into two jerks, humiliating me at every opportunity; they never practiced the ethics of care Jesus called his followers to do in the Parable of the Good Samaritan.

Wherever we went, people were impressed by our size and strength, and there was no place we needed both more than in the two months we gutted homes effected by Hurricane Katrina. Fr. John Languish missioned us to New Orleans, to experience poverty and to work with Catholic Charities. We stayed at the parish of the Immaculate Conception on Baronne Street. Because Matt was so much older and always complaining of ailments, Kris agreed to bunk with me in a two-bed bedroom. I so wanted them to offer me the single room occupancy, but instead, I had to share close quarters with someone who neither spoke to me, nor wished to know me. To be clear, Matt and Kris, had stopped speaking with me after I came out during the telling of vocation stories way back in August 2005. Human beings are social animals, with rational appetites, and desires for socialization; Matt and Kris denied me the capacity to flourish (so much for emulating our Lord!), and our Novice Master was many, many miles away.

When we went out to gut houses, I mixed in with anyone I could; it was as if I came up into fresh air, I could breathe, I could speak to the living, and they would listen. I started to gain weight immediately, working hard by using a sledgehammer, going for long walks through the French Quarter, walking as slowly as I could through the Gay neighborhood. I was too afraid to enter a gay bar alone, too afraid because I knew in my loneliness that I would likely strike up a conversation with a hot guy and look to hook-up. I passed by gay bar after gay bar, for it wasn't so much sex I wanted but friendship. Or so I had convinced myself.

When Matt threw his back out, Kris and I worked the usual Katrina-rotted out shot gun built home. All around us was death, lifeless plants, ruined bushes, destroyed homes: New Orleans was a wasteland. We found homes infested with salted cockroaches living and breeding, such was the life of these extremely poor, vulnerable, and mostly African-American people. We found fallen pictures of loved ones, refrigerators still full with food, battered desk lamps, kids' homework notebooks, boxes of bullets, sexual vibrators, a teenage son's porno collection, video games, washing machines, stockings, sneakers, now the debris of a lifetime.

We gutted the homes to their core, hoping that someone would come later and restore them to life. It was as if by gutting these homes, I hoped to bring my relationship with Matt and Kris to life. Working alone with Kris was easily a trial. I tried to talk to him, made every effort to be open and friendly but to no avail. I also prayed that Matt would return, just so I could overhear them talking. I liked silence, but not the silence of denial and rejection.

Matt only returned to work because the Novice Master had ordered him, "If you don't get back to work, I'll dismiss you." Matt had already overstayed his welcome, telling anyone he could his theory of urban planning, his vision for New Orleans. Matt's theory, was "in the spirit and guise of the Great Mongol Emperor Genghis Khan, turn everything in sight into a plate of glass and then pave over it." To Matt the materially poor would always be with us, and he had no intention to prove it wrong. Sometimes I imagined myself shaking Tweedledee and Tweedledum, wanting so much to put some of Jesus' love and kindness into them. I couldn't tell if they were a pair of clowns, or just a pair of man's men who'd spend the rest of their lives wounding others.

There were a few lighter moments during our trip. On the way home one afternoon, Kris dropped us off at the local dive bar, near a cemetery. We entered the bar, I looked it over, and started to smile. It was worse than a gay bar, it was a leather bar! But because Kris survived Romania, I guess, he decided he could stay, beat the odds or prove his manhood, and have one can of Budweiser. When a rail-thin shirtless bartender asked Kris what he wanted, he mumbled "beer," then caught himself and said, "a Bud." Then, a hefty, leather vested man sat next to Matt; the bartender served him the usual and started to exchange pleasantries with the only guy for thousands of miles to have a degree from the Pontifical Lateran University. When I stopped trying to figure out the bar's theme, I turned to see who had caught Matt's attention; under the man's hairy armpit sat a furry Chihuahua! Feeling protective of Matt, I paid our bill and we left.

Next, Tweedledee, Tweedledum and I were missioned to Calvary Hospital in the Bronx, where we'd work as Cancer Care Technicians, for our hospital experiment. This time, rather than share a bedroom with Kris as we had in New Orleans we each had our own room in Loyola Hall on the campus of Fordham University. I had to work with Matt on the same floor. By this time, I secretly wondered if Fr. John Languish wanted me out of the Novitiate.

When other Jesuits asked me about my classmates, I couldn't really say anything about them, and slowly word was getting around that my two classmates were intolerant jerks. I told the truth as I saw it to the Novice Master, about my experiences, going weekends without their speaking to me, being uninvited to social events, driving in the car in dead silence. Once, when I was both so exhausted from being treated like crap by Matt and Kris, and after a particularly hard day of working with people near death, I drove our Toyota Sienna van home recklessly, and fast, nearly losing the left side view mirror. It had been days since I heard them speak; when Kris said, "Slow down," I felt seething rage, but I rammed it in; it felt as if I were the victim of sexual orientation harassment. I didn't sign up to be ostracized by two men who hated gay people! Where was the camaraderie, the companionship that Fr. Paul Arnold and Fr. Jerry Mettlesome promised that I'd easily find in the Jesuit community? Some of my older, gay Jesuit friends were miles or states away, more calls for spiritual conversation wouldn't help.

In fact, on many occasions between February and May 2006, I almost left the Jesuits because I felt worthless. But I was more and more confident that God would help me weather this storm, that if I reached out to Him from the boat, like Peter, that His Son Jesus would grab hold of me and lead me to safety. I often prayed for such a divine intervention during private masses with the traditional theologian Avery Cardinal Dulles, who at the time lived on the campus of Fordham University.

To weather the storm of being on the road with Kris and Matt, I thought about the images of God I discerned during the Long Retreat, a God who loves me, one who says to me, "My beloved son." I prayed for the LGBTQ youth whom I wanted to serve, for whom I tolerated the torments of Kris and Matt. That's when my short term goal was to get through these experiments, to get back to the Novitiate, to be fed by other, more nourishing friendships. I needed to bear it for only a little bit longer.

Soon we did return, and the second year men came back from their long experiments. There were more conferences, more long dinners, more stories. Syracuse is a beautiful city in the spring, with her rising hills, trees and glorious sun. We didn't stay long; against Fr. John Languish's wishes we were headed to the Jesuits-in-formation conference in California. We arrived at Loyola Marymount University, located just outside Los Angeles. It was a paradise, whose vistas were impressive and inviting, and whose climate and weather mirrored the colors of a Van Gogh painting.

It was also about this time that I learned that Jesuits throw the biggest bashes of any religious order. Aside from the expense of the traveling—all the men from various parts of the country, some 200 plus men—there was the expense of food, beverage, lodging, gas, and recreational activities; we even received tickets to attend an Anaheim Angels game.

I shared an apartment with a Canadian Jesuit named Myles Love. Each day he paraded around our apartment in a towel, with no underwear; I could tell, because his body was toned, and my eyes followed the hair from his belly button down to his pubic hairs. He shaved his face every day, even when he had no facial hair.

I met many gay Jesuits, including some African-American Jesuits in formation, and wondered what they thought of white privilege, and how hard it must be to be a gay, African-American man in formation.

I socialized with many men, but at night I stayed in, as I was too psychologically wounded from my months with Tweedledee and Tweedledum. I missed opportunities to stay up late to get to know young men in formation whom I admired, like Andrew Soon-Yee, the Chinese American Jesuit who interviewed me at Xavier High School. He asked me the toughest questions, yet he didn't ask me about my sexual preferences. A red flag went up in my mind because I expected that since I was openly gay that we might discuss homosexuality and the priesthood. This was, after all, something we might share in common. I said nothing. As the Austrian-British philosopher Ludwig Wittgenstein said, "Whereof one cannot speak, thereof one must remain silent."

While some men found this conference energizing, including the discussions with Provincials about province realignment, or meta questions about strategic planning, others like me found it too idealistic. Moreover, I wanted my Novice Master to be there, so that I could speak with him about that disambiguating conversation he had with me just before we left for California. I wanted to have him clarify his comments, comments that were so hurtful, so untimely, so deleterious that I had asked every gay Jesuit I met what he meant. Indeed, some days before we left, when Fr. John Languish was in a foul mood, and perhaps tired by my reporting negative experiences with Kris and Matt, he finally told me that I had erred, making the fundamental mistake in coming out, and that a class of three is hard enough without someone's adding human sexuality to the mix. Even when I met Catholic priests during the sacrament of reconciliation they encouraged me to be myself and to find peace in God's love and forgiveness. Fr. John Languish was telling me not to be angry, not to be so transparent, or honest. Why was I wrong? I simply wanted to reflect publicly the very person God loved me to be, and to be that person honestly as a Roman Catholic priest.

Fr. John Languish derided me, "In August you should've come to me before acting so stridently, so impulsively"; he added, "not all the men in your community will be your friends" and "coming out in a forum like that isn't prudent." He went on, that had his mom not died, he would've had us share our stories together during a mid-July meeting, which would've been our litmus test.

Again, a Catholic priest was telling me that I, a gay man, whom God had confirmed time and again as God's beloved, was disordered, disoriented and utterly misguided. I had done wrong, not Kris or Matt. To Fr. John Languish I had to take the moral higher ground by being silent, not honest, they could be safe in their homophobia, and I hysterical because of my anger. To him, my classmates had done no wrong. To him, they still bore the standard of Christ as defined by St. Ignatius of Loyola. It was I who hadn't discerned correctly truth-telling, honesty, or being. The more Fr. John spoke, the more enervated I felt. I finally mustered the courage to ask, Why did you wait nine-months to tell me this? He replied that, Because now you are ready, now you are strong enough, now you can hear it. When he asked me, Anything else, Ben?, I said No and retired to my twin bed.

When I went back to my room, I saw a black and white photo I had developed in my high school senior year photography class, the image of a cross I had taken from several feet above, an aerial shot, taken in a hamlet outside Paris. I saw myself kneeling before Christ crucified, then imagining what Christ himself saw, as in the *Crucifixion, seen from the Cross* by the nineteenth century French genre painter James Tissot. Then I was reminded of Jesus' final seven words, *Eloi Eloi lama Sabachthani,* "My God, My God, why have You Forsaken Me?" That night God seemed so distant from me. I felt so alone.

After California, the Novice Master missioned us to Cochabamba, Bolivia. Yes, this is what we do, we go to ravaged towns, cities, countries, where people are in desperate need, the very people for whom Pope Francis I washes feet. And I was so willing to do so because I was in a position to help people, which is a part of being a novice and a priest: We live not for the self but for Christ and for those He loves, and He loves everyone.

We were also to study and to learn Spanish. Thankfully, Fr. Languish didn't have a capacity for Spanish, deciding instead to prepare the unruly second-year men for their profession of vows. Apparently they required more formation after their six-month internships in Jesuit apostolates. As such, Fr. Languish missioned his assistant, Fr. Jerry Conscience to go to Bolivia with us. Without Fr. Jerry, the Cristo statute, the hummingbirds, the Jesuit Reductions and the poor and generous people of Bolivia, I wouldn't have lasted as long as I did in the Jesuits.

While in Bolivia Fr. Jerry and I became friends; he pastorally cared for me, as we bonded over music by Neil Young, Mark Knopfler and Em-mylou Harris, also bonding over the Bolivian cuisine, and cheap taxi rides; we walked to and from school at the Maryknoll Center for Languages in Cochabamba. We took local buses and toured the market (La Cancha). Fr. Jerry rehabilitated me to community life, helping me trust members of the Society of Jesus again and telling stories about his formation, about an older Jesuits who had died from HIV/AIDS; he had essentially taken my mind off of Matt and Kris and Fr. John Languish. In doing so he became a hero to me.

I prayed to the Cristo statue every afternoon. I'd spend the hour of daily prayer staring at Jesus, some hundreds of feet tall, with arms wide open to the world. I watched as the smog lifted and abated, or hung snuggly around it, an ever changing Christ, ever present, ever reaching out to us, to me a gay man, to tell me He loves me, offering me the courage to go on.

Sometimes green hummingbirds or bees would distract me, but like gravitational pull, my eyes and heart turned to Him, and He gave me rest. I longed to be wrapped in His embrace, for His arms to enfold, to enclose and to protect me. The more I prayed, the more I heard, "Be a Jesuit priest, do this for me." I believed it, more than believed it. I was one with Christ, and I wanted to please Him.

It now is clear to me: In those youthful days I was (and still am) in love with Jesus Christ. It's so simple, so obvious to me now, but I was at the time so caught in dark confusion and stress that I failed to see how much in love I was.

It was for Christ that I was here, why I put up with Kris and Matt when I sometimes wanted to knock the shit out of them, with one good right hook. As a fan of the WWE, I sometimes imagined giving them the Rock Bottom, the famous finishing move by Dwayne "the Rock" Johnson. But it was the Cristo statue that reoriented me toward what mattered most. I was very moved by what the authors of the Jesuit General Congregation 31 wrote about in Document 14,

> Our entire spiritual life is in Christ Jesus. We share, of course, the adoptive sonship of God which all the faithful have through faith and baptism, but belong in a special way to God through our consecration as religious in the Society. . .This very intimacy with Christ forges a union of our life of prayer and our life of apostolic work. Far from living two separate lives, we are strengthened and guided towards action in our prayer while our action in turn urges us to pray.

Whether it was the twice-daily Examination of Conscience that I adapted to my particular circumstances (*e.g.*, rejection by my classmates, or attendance at daily liturgy in Spanish) the time I spent with Jesus grew in me, allowing a blossoming of an awareness and self-knowledge about my status in the Society of Jesus that I would return to the Novitiate and recommit to "vowed" life.

The next year flew by though I didn't experience the reconciliation with Fr. John Languish, Kris or Matt that I had hoped for. Soon, though I accepted the fact that as they grew closer, I'd grow further apart from them.

My attention fell upon an angelic looking Novice who arrived at the Novitiate, with whom I'd spend more and more time as the year went on. Earl Smart was a blue eyed, blond haired New Englander whose eyes spoke about pain, about which I would learn more.

His favorite saint was the twelfth century writer Aelred of Rievaulx, whose text, *On Spiritual Friendship* he'd refer to as much as I referred to the theologian Karl Rahner's seminal work, *The Spiritual Exercises* or Johannes Baptist Metz's spiritual text, *Poverty of Spirit*. Earl and I also loved Hermann Hesse, though we chose different texts, he, *Narcissus and Goldmund* and I, *Siddhartha*: The former about the love of a monk for his pupil, the latter about a young man's trying to understand the suffering of the world.

We couldn't bond over music, since Earl liked German music and I rock. I did turn Earl on to the band Toad and the Wet Sprocket, music we'd both jog to; sometimes we'd run to the nearby glacier formed lake called Green Lake.

That summer, in 2007, three months before Tweedledee, Tweedledum and I professed vows, we novices went to Denver for the "Novice History Month." In the mile high city, Earl and I reveled in our budding friendship, though neither of us at the time understood that it was a romance. We hiked up mountains, drank at night, avoided secret meetings and gatherings of gay men and our allies in formation. These gay novices had heard about the cruelty of my classmates, and wanted to support me, to rally behind me, but I knew, by that second year on the Novice Master's Plantation, that one was neither a white, black, gay, straight, smart, dumb, jock, geek, tall or short Jesuit, one was only a Jesuit. It didn't matter either if one was a scholastic, brother or priest. To Fr. Languish *Magis* (more) meant life in Christ first and foremost. Yet Christ himself is not color-blind, gender-blind or sexuality-blind. When someone purports to be blind to color, gender or sexuality they are being counterproductive, thus ignoring discrimination and reproducing inequality.

Towards the end of the summer, the actor Bill Murray visited Regis University, where he had apparently completed some study before turning to acting full time. The night he arrived Regis threw a splash of a party, open bar, food, the works. When the Jesuit novices got wind of it, we migrated towards the other part of campus. Excessive drink and socializing are commonplace in Jesuit life. On a given day, the Jesuit community will gather for mass at 5:30pm, then socialize until 6:15pm, which is followed by dinner. During this time the Jesuits (and their guests) will pour themselves libations, usually blended scotch, and eat assorted cheeses and salted meats. In brief, it's a long cocktail hour.

In Denver, the novices cherished "social nights"; it was an opportunity to release the boredom from the week of study, and every weekend each Novitiate was charged with putting on a social. The California Province chose a Mexican theme, with pina coladas and margaritas, the Missouri and Wisconsin Provinces an Oktoberfest. The one in which St. Andrew Hall was placed in charge was a huge hit with the other novices. For the theme, we selected the Cohen Brother's film *The Big Lebowski*. In some ways nihilism was appropriate given our sexual sublimations. Fr. John Languish wanted me, my fellow Long Islander and first year novice, Maud Perspicacious, to throw, and organize our Novitiate's "social night." As Jeff Bridges tells us in that movie, *The Dude Abides*, and Maud and I desired nothing more than to mix white Russians and make Fr. John happy.

The night Bill Murray visited campus Maud Perspicacious learned about it through the "SIN Network" (the Scholastic Information Network, aka the gossip line); he made an effort to meet his favorite actor, also star of *Ghostbusters*. That night after many drinks, Earl and I wandered off, taking up residence on a bench overlooking the Rocky Mountains. It was a glorious night. Then we started sharing intimate details about our lives again, I was inebriated, not sure about Earl, and his tolerance was surprising. Then we were telling each other that we loved one another, while my arm was around his shoulder. Earl pushed me away, said I was drunk. I asked him not to tell Fr. Languish. He agreed.

When we returned to Syracuse, we prepared for our home visits, then a week's vacation together at the Jesuit villa house in Cape May, Maryland. It was there, during those hot summer days, that Earl and I would begin drinking alone together, into the morning together. Then one night we drank bottles of Chimay (a Belgian beer) together. A Jesuit priest who was staying with us, as the "Father in charge" of the villa, saw us one night, as we sat alone and popped open another bottle of Chimay. He said, *be careful*. But, by then, Earl and I were linked, and as we finished our beers, we left for one last night swim before our morning departure.

Earl and I made it to the beach, then Earl ran into the water. I laughed from my belly and couldn't believe it. I didn't go in because I was too afraid. I started snapping pictures. Then Earl and I climbed a nearby lifeguard stand, and looking out over the ocean. The moon, stars and stillness of the night, the quiet, longing, rumbling of the ocean, the waves, all of it proved too inviting to us.

During that unforgettable night, our affection for each other could not be contained, his for me nor mine for him. Affection? Dare I say love?

As we returned to Syracuse, Earl and I did what we thought was prudent; we told Fr. John Languish and Fr. Jerry Conscience about our mutual self-realization that we might be or actually were in love. We left out the details, opting for rational thoughts and sentiments over irrational actions and impulses. Fr. John and Fr. Jerry seemed convinced that Earl and I had fallen in love, and that only distance would mend this tide. While Fr. John wished he could keep me in the Novitiate, he knew that I'd profess vows, and depart the Novitiate. On some level, both Fr. John and I understood that my actions may also have reflected a desire to cause Fr. John pain.

I may have wanted to hurt Fr. John because he had done nothing to end my experience: of hatred, humiliation, and homophobia at the hands of Tweedledee and Tweedledum. Over those two years with Tweedledee and Tweedledum, I learned a lot about victimization and re-victimization. I learned also that there are many unkind, if not cruel, men who still receive permission to be ordained. Men who might not have been be ordained if the Church allowed kind and generous married men to seek the sacrament. (By this point in my tenure with Kris and Matt I wondered: if they left the Jesuits would they just become lost souls?)

On August 11, 2007 I professed vows along with Kris and Matt. It took me by surprise that Fr. John Languish called Kris, Matt and me "a blessed trinity"! Where did he find that metaphor in the readings selected for our Vow Mass, which included the prophet Jeremiah (1:4–10, 17–10), St. Paul's Letter to the Philippians (2:1–11) and the Gospel According to St. John (15:9–17)? So many parts of the reading countered my experiences of Kris and Matt over the two years; from them there was no mercy, no love, no compassion. I found comfort in these readings also knowing that I had not had a nervous breakdown while on the road with Tweedledee and Tweedledum.

That night, after the families and friends retreated to their hotels, Earl and I met in the kitchen. Earl had waited for me. That week he and I had made a rite of going to the campus of Le Moyne and gazing at the heavens and the hosts. Sometimes we held each other's hands, sometimes we kissed, sometimes we rolled around in the grass by the gym. When we returned to St. Andrew Hall, I cursed our twin beds. On August 11, 2007 I was a newly vowed Jesuit, and Earl remained a novice.

Days later, I interrogated all that had transpired against the conclusion to my First Vows Paper, where I had articulated my understanding of my desire to respond to God's invitation to be a Jesuit priest, reflecting on the vows of poverty, chastity and obedience. I wrote,

> In the end, the vows of chastity, poverty and obedience unite the newly professed Jesuit in mind, body and soul with others, to a community of friends in the Lord, as well as to the poor who long for *this world* to live in solidarity with them in generosity, love and humility. The vows of chastity, poverty and obedience foster the mission of the Society today, a mission that is apostolically objective, aiming itself toward the creation of the Kingdom of God for our human society. My own personal desire to profess perpetual vows of chastity, poverty and obedience answers God's calling me to freely, humbly and lovingly live out my own Baptismal creational principle and foundation. By professing perpetual vows of chastity, poverty obedience, I act out of complete and perfect love, finding the initiative in grace and nature, to courageously choose a Jesuit life always ready for more.

It is no wonder that on my Vow Day my voice quavered. I was torn between two goods, life with another man, maybe Earl, and life as a professed member of the Society of Jesus.

St. Augustine says, "Love and do what you will." Freedom was coming, oh yes, oh freedom was coming, oh yes, I know. Or so I hoped.

Chapter 8

Backdoor to the East

As a diehard Yankees fan, I knew some *cool* sports facts about St. Louis, the Catholic city known as the Gateway to the West. I knew the Yankees catcher and baseball hall of famer Yogi Berra was born here, on The Hill. I knew the Yankees lost the 1964 World Series to the St. Louis Cardinals. It was also Micky Mantle's last series. The Yankees wouldn't appear in a World Series until 1976. Growing up, I was also a fan of Brett Hull and the St. Louis Blues, perhaps because I played the saxophone in high school, though my attempts at Jazz were futile. Fr. John Languish also studied in St. Louis, where he became a huge fan of the Cardinals.

St. Louis was one of four sites the newly professed (vowed) Jesuits went to continue their formation; the others were Chicago, the Bronx, and Toronto. Each Philosophate or First Studies program included the rigorous pursuit of a philosophy degree, while some, like St. Louis afforded the men greater flexibility, *e.g.*, completing a chemistry degree and the requisite philosophy credits needed to be ordained in the Roman Catholic Church.

I had avoided Fordham University because the program was the most inflexible; in fact, it was termed "the Flat Earth Program" because Jesuits studied traditional theological doctrine, and dogma. Many younger Jesuits studied in doctoral courses with students who were far more talented than they. Gone were the days of "Jesuit privilege" and "Jesuit superiority."

The Flat Earth Program included academic courses in Greek and Latin, and few electives; the majority of one's time was spent in Medieval Philosophy, a time that looked to nip sinful cultural problems in the bud, before thought turned from vice to habit. The First Studies Program at

Fordham attempted to sell Medieval Philosophy as a true substitute for Jesus' advocation for taking charge of one's spiritual inner life in the Sermon on the Mount. Why debate faith versus reason? No thank you Boethius, St. Anselm, Duns Scotus, William of Ockham, and Thomas Aquinas. I didn't buy it!

The poet W.H. Auden said there was an excess of reason, and too little place for the irrational, revelation and mystery in God's cosmos. No book, no theory, no philosophy will help me understand people, how to help the needy, how to be compassionate and empathetic. And the very idea of being involved in a theological debate with anyone is repugnant to me. All I needed was to stand in awe before every person I met, each an enigma, each fraught with divinity, each his/her own divinization the Holy Trinity. (Hadn't Fr. John referred to me, Kris and Matt as his Blessed Trinity in his sermon from our Vow Day liturgy!)

Sometimes a Jesuit Scholastic could take a theology class or two, to expedite the four-year theology requirement for ordination. The young Jesuit Scholastics I knew avoided the controversial female theologians Elizabeth Johnson, C.S.J. and Jeannine Hill Fletcher; they wouldn't go near women who referred to God as "She" or who invited them to consider motherhood as a metaphor for interreligious dialogue. Further, studying the works of theologians like Mary Daly or Elisabeth Schussler Fiorenza was considered profane and secular, not sacrosanct or inviolable.

I chose Saint Louis University as the site to complete my graduate degree in social work, and to be able to meet fellow Jesuits whom I admired, e.g., the spiritual author of many works on Ignatian Spirituality, Fr. Dave Fleming, the historian; Fr. John Padberg, the philosopher; Fr. John Kavanaugh and the liturgist; Fr. John Foley, a member of the famous Christian music group, The St. Louis Jesuits. In addition, I'd be able to mix in with my Secundi, Tyler-no-plain-clothes, Jolly and Paddy O'Toolihan. I'd also be able to meet and spend time with the east coast Jesuits only African-American Scholastic Martin Powder. I'd also reunite with Gianni Remington, a Jamaican Jesuit who completed the Long Retreat with me at the Gonzaga Eastern Point Retreat House.

I arrived in St. Louis on a typical summer afternoon; it was humid, and I mean humid, it was as if I stood before a blow dryer, with all that hot, moist air blowing in my face. I drove from Syracuse with the Bishop. Much of the time I was secretly a wreck, my inner life full of crying, pining, lusting, desiring, enamoring, hoping and loving. My thoughts were still on Earl, and whether or not I had made the prudent (right) choice, though still very much freely, to profess First Vows. I already started pondering the benefits of voluntary celibacy. Still, when asked, I would have highlighted availability as a benefit of the denial of human relationship. I wasn't deluded, I was honest: yes, I had had an affair with Earl, but so many married couples seek reconciliation and renewal of their vows; separation and divorce are not inevitable. Perhaps, I was, as St. Paul thought, overwhelmed by my passions. Yet, such ruminations would be short lived that day because I met Malcolm Boyd.

Malcolm Boyd answered the door, and I believe it was love at first sight. He stood at 6foot 1inch, with a ruddy face, soft, watery blue eyes and smooth lips. His body matched his handsome face, strong looking legs, powerful hips, a slim, strong torso. I thought of the statue of Michelangelo's *David*. He was a fine specimen. I'm being very romantic in my memory of Malcolm, I know, but it's how I felt when I first met him. He also gave me a good look-over. I was pleased that maybe he was as attracted to me as I him. I told him who I was, and he gave me that laugh that would drive me wonderfully crazy for the next academic year.

The Bishop helped me bring my belongings into my room, which was the smallest living quarters, the place I'd eventually call home. Then we left, for a brief stay in Chicago, where the Bishop studied philosophy and theology and received the title of "Super Beadle" of the complicated Scholastic network attached to the Jesuit community of Loyola University. The Bishop represented the Church and the Society of Jesus too well, I wondered if he disagreed with anything, or whether or not he was capable of criticizing the Church or the Society of Jesus.

I often wondered if he were gay. And if so, could he work in an archdiocesan school? Could he teach the required chapters on morality? Could he look his students in the eye? And if he couldn't, would he have the courage to quit in protest? One thing I knew already: there are few, if any, young Bishops who dissent. It falls to the laity to quit, to resign, to protest, or far worse.

I left the Bishop and Super Beadle to rule over his fiefdom, taking the Megabus back to St. Louis.

Once back in my room, Earl and I continued our communications; there were emails, hand-written letters and phone calls. My phone bill ran up so much that the Jesuit priest in charge of paying the bills, a middle-aged man, asked me if I were an extrovert, when he really wanted to know, "Who the hell are you calling?" In St. Louis, the Scholastics earned slightly more per month, some $150.00, which money was used for personal expenses, not including food from the local grocery store, called Schnuck's, or gas. As Jesuits, we had "unlimited" gas cards. Sure, one was to monitor his use of benefactor's money, but to us, unlimited meant: Let's get off campus!

My next superior was a Jesuit filled with more rage than King Lear; he was a man who made intemperate outbursts against men he deemed too conservative, men who didn't sanctify the El Salvadorian Jesuit Martyrs. Donald Mercurial was a double Ivy League alum, who seemed to feel imprisoned by his mission as Rector of the Bellarmine House of Studies, named after the Saint and Doctor of the Church, Cardinal Robert Bellarmine. The First Studies program produced many good Jesuits, who like Bellarmine were men of the Counter-Reformation.

I could see stress in Fr. Mercurial's face. I could also see that he liked Malcolm, often telling us sarcastic, but funny, stories about running into him at the swimming pool. And I realized that he was a lonely man. I wished he could swim without thinking, believing exercise might give him an outlet, but he couldn't relax.

Mercurial had his favorite scholastics, with whom he may have found some release from the duress of his assignment. To be homo-social, Mercurial was friendly with Riley Gansavort, a New Orleans Province Jesuit, whose mood was always positive, and whose puppy-dog eyes never vacillated; he was neither too hot, nor too cold. There were other men he sought friendship with, not many his peers, young Jesuits like Ronald Maybe, Andrew Van Sand and Matthew Knotts, men with whom he'd go to Brennan's or the Scottish Arms and drink back a few top shelf single malts.

Even before my affair with Malcolm Boyd climaxed, Mercurial and I never got along. While I preferred the narrative, he desired facts. While I favored communication and vulnerability, he wanted stoicism and equations. While I studied history, he labored in economics.

Earl was always on my mind. I loved him, I missed him, I wanted him. I had to tell someone about him or I'd burst. I knew Martin Powder was very sympathetic, I had always seen him at big Jesuit gatherings with his white pals, Greg Cappuccino and Jared Karp.

I chose Martin, and one airy, late summer night, we walked through the streets of St. Louis, with my telling him everything about Earl and me.

I am more than thankful for Martin's place in my life; without him, at that moment of crisis, I might have jumped ship. For the secrets of my affair with Earl ate at me, and I couldn't tell Malcolm Boyd, because I didn't want to rebound. I wanted to return to balance, to that state of being St. Ignatius of Loyola addresses, one that restores the person to the right relationship with God, self and others. In short, my aim was, and had always been, to be a whole person, who successfully lives voluntary chastity, poverty and obedience. I am of a mind that even my scars, my losses, my failures, my wounds, all will in the end lead me to wholeness; they would also lead me to ultimate wholeness in Christ, as the American poet Samuel Menashe writes in his poem *Cargo*,

Old wounds leave good hollows
Where one who goes can hold
Himself in ghostly embraces
Of former powers and graces
Whose domain no strife mars—
I am made whole by my scars
For whatever now displaces
Follows all that once was
And without loss stows
Me into my own spaces

Martin also helped me to know Fr. Donald Mercurial better, and to build up the courage to meet with him. Our first meeting was extremely awkward, as if neither of us spoke English, or as if Ludwig Wittgenstein had us both right, he whose aim in *Tractatus* includes: "what can be said (language) about it (the world), and what can only be shown."

I poured out my heart to him, telling him that I had fallen in love, and that I truly, deeply, desired to remain a Jesuit. I wept, and told I him was in turmoil; I said the person I loved was many states away. Donald said, "Ben, you are a Jesuit now," and that "Jesuits fall in love; we will deal with this as adults." Then, like my dad would often do, he fell into silence. I begged him to speak, but he remained silent.

Earl and I had been losing touch, physically, emotionally and geographically. Then we had to come clean and face the facts: To Earl, this affair was simply that; he wanted to be a Jesuit, a son of Ignatius. I was ambivalent, but I said that if he'd leave the Jesuits, then I'd go with him.

Life is about taking risks, while the only certainty is death - that is for sure. Earl did not want to take the risk to jump ship with me; for that choice I have no resentment or anger for him.

As the dust of our relationship settled, I looked to fit into my new community. I finally took a deep breath, started praying again, working out, running, and studying. I visited all of St. Louis' "acronymic" museums, I went to the SLUMA, SLAM, and MOCRA. I mixed in at Karen House, the local Catholic Worker House that served female victims of violence and their children. I went to mass at an African-American, Jesuit run parish, St. Matthew the Apostle. I saw firsthand what a dying parish looked like. It was as if St. Matthew's itself suffered from Chronic Obstructive Pulmonary Disease (COPD), and was dying a slow and painful death.

St. Louis was a war zone, the result of decades of racism and white supremacy.

At the Bellarmine House of Studies, the Scholastics left their Victorianesque, St. Louis red brick, homes and walked down Westminster Place.

At the corner of the street, just before the behemoth known as the St. Louis City Masonic Temple, Scholastics decide to turn left or right. If you turn left, you enter the poor, black ghetto almost immediately. There you find abandoned buildings, crumbling from the lack of life, from poverty and from lack of maintenance; you hear gun shots; you hear the music of Marvin Gaye, rap and hip hop; you smell outdoor catfish fry during Lent; you see kids riding bikes in the heat, and Chrysler's with twenty-two-inch rims the color of eggplant and lime green. Still such a segregated city, Saint Louis was the site of the failed public housing complex Pruitt-Igoe. The failure of public housing across our country is not a myth.

If you turn right, you enter the safe world of the St. Louis University Billikens, a student body that is sheltered by campus gates, and Campus Ministry life. On Sunday night, at St. Francis Xavier Parish, the Campus Ministry team turned the 10pm student mass into a performance fit for Disney World's Epcot Center.

To the right, there was also poverty, poverty of spirit, much less marginal, but still very much a part of the predominately white, undergraduate body at St. Louis University. Like most Jesuit Universities and Colleges, St. Louis University was impoverishing her students by raising tuition. What undergraduate wouldn't need Medicaid, Medicare or food stamps, if they didn't live with their parents or have a job after graduation? What's $50,000 times four? The Jesuit Scholastics paid their tuition through the generosity of benefactors and stewards. Many of them were LGBTQ people, but while their treasure is taken, the Church increasingly tells them that their time and talent are not needed. Perhaps ironically, the Jesuits accepted (needed) me, an at-the-time closeted gay man to continue on towards priesthood - and thus, I remained on track for ordination in a Church that rejected as "objectively disordered" men and women who identified freely as LGBTQ.

As the fall went on, and as I mixed in more and more with Jesuit Scholastics at what's called the "Fourth House," I took in a life of fraternizing that Fr. John Languish had so painfully tried to eliminate. The Fourth House was run by our assistant rector, the young, charming, Marlboro Man, named Dick Subterfuge. Dick was a generous boy from Kansas, whose dad worked as a corrections officer. He had a fun accent, chain smoked, drove a Buick, worked as often and as long as he could, and when the weekend came, he released his energy with us "kids" because there was absolutely no one his age whom he didn't feel threatened by, or who wasn't damaged by the great exodus of men from formation following Vatican II and leading through the 1990s. Some say in any given class, 50% plus of the men will leave. Dick, was perhaps the only survivor. He would entertain us boys, telling Jesuit war stories while we sucked down beer, DiGiorno's pizzas and crunched on salted chips. The Fourth House was essentially a Frat House, and once the music got going, it didn't stop.

For a time I couldn't believe these activities were what young celibate men did to pass the time, to cope with a lack of relationships, to seek camaraderie and relationships with other Type-A men. Malcolm Boyd lived at the Fourth House. I had succeeded in implementing what I called my Safety Plan. I refused to be alone with Malcolm because I sensed our mutual attraction. I knew I wasn't in the right frame of mind to entertain healthy boundaries with a young Jesuit who entered religious life right out of high school.

Each opportunity we had, however, saw us spending more time together. We'd chat each other up while cleaning up after dinner, or I'd stay a little longer with him in one of the reading rooms, or we'd bike ride alone to his grandmother's house or to the St. Louis Botanical Gardens.

I did try my best to keep my attraction to Malcolm at bay. And for a time it worked. Soon, though, Malcolm started copying my dress, wearing ties on the days I wore ties, corduroys when I wore them. Though he hardly called, he did show up at my bedroom, whittling down the boundaries. Then he started asking me about love, and one day, while at the St. Louis Botanical Gardens, we gazed upward at strikingly puffy and white cumulus nimbus clouds. He told me about men he'd "slipped" with as a Jesuit. Malcolm and I lay on the grass, nearly touching, on the blankets he brought. As he described his terminally ill grandmother and her influence on him, I was triggered by empathy, as I was with Earl.

I too played a role, that is for sure, but I was also worn down by my studies, my prayer life, drinking heavily at the Fourth House, taxed even further by another young Jesuit, Jack Broussard who'd come out to me, and told me that I was the first and only Jesuit to know. Jack said Mercurial had recommended that he speak with me, that I was an integrated, young gay Jesuit, who could be trusted and to whom Jack could confide. I finally felt validated! (It was ironic, Mercurial celebrated me for being a model gay person and peer despite my all-too-recent history of failing at celibacy. In religious life, I'd be a model gay person, but out of the order I'd be sinning and need forgiveness and reconciliation every time I had intercourse. Ironic no, hypocrisy, yes.) Our friendship was strong, until Jack fell in love with me. He then sent me a letter ending our friendship. I was stunned to say the least. I started thinking, would anyone who knew about the inner world of religious life have anything positive to say about voluntary celibacy? I lamented, why do so many inexperienced gay Catholic men opt for the collar of the priesthood?

The winter came and went; it was now 2008; someone, as a joke, had given me a Vietnam era gas mask as a gift during our Christmas exchange. I could've heeded the metaphor because that winter and spring I entered a breathless, sordid love affair: Malcolm and Ben. It started one weekend, when Malcolm and I went to the Green Hills Villa House for a respite. The small house was crowded with other Scholastics, so we opted to stay at the big house, rather than return home.

The Big House had one room with two double beds in it. Malcolm said let's stay here. We began our emotional affair. We became inseparable. We fought cattily. We made up. Then one night we found ourselves alone at the Fourth House. Malcolm and I were joined by Dick Subterfuge and his minion Rory O'Grady, a young Jesuit from the Missouri Province. They too were drunk, but all they did was look from Malcolm to me to the television to each other. They stood there. It seemed like an eternity. After they left, Malcolm's hand started to caress my arm. Then his hands closed in on mine. We were in each other's arms before long. Then Malcolm was on top of me, kissing me. We removed our shirts, then our underwear, then our sneakers. We were drunk. That night we did not have sex, but we did come very close. Afterwards Malcolm told me that he was in a twelve-step recovery program for sexaholics! I was incredulous.

We cleaned up, as best we could, then slept on the basement couches. Exhausted? No, relieved. When 6 am arrived, Martin Powder showed up. What the hell was he doing here? In the basement of the Fourth House, at 6 am? Martin and I both lived at Second House. I overheard, as if from a fugue state, Martin and Malcolm's arguing. It was all like a scene from James Baldwin's gay novel *Giovanni's Room*.

The next three months included psychological warfare between Malcolm and Martin, psychological dependency, and longing between Martin and me. Each of us played the silent game with the other. I told everything about what had happened to Fr. Dick Subterfuge, who was in charge since Fr. Donald Mercurial was off in Rome participating in the Jesuit General Congregation Thirty-Five, where he would help elect the next Superior General.

Fr. Dick said, Ben, who could resist, you are so exotic. Yikes! I was stunned, but Dick was way over his head in this role as acting rector. He himself had survived the carnal realities of the "Fuse Box," the nickname of the residence hall he lived in when he was a young Scholastic. Dick would tell wild and crazy stories about men dressing in drag for Halloween, or sunbathing nude on the roof. No wonder Dick turned to modern art and to curating museums.

When Mercurial returned, we had a new Superior General, Fr. Adolfo Nicholas, and new decrees, like *A Fire that Enkindles Other Fires, Challenges to Our Mission Today: Sent to the Frontiers* and *Obedience in the Life of the Society of Jesus*. I immediately asked for a meeting with Mercurial to disclose the details of my affair with Malcolm. Mercurial surmised that Malcolm had initiated sex with me. He said, "his libido is strong." I'll say, but so is mine!

As Fr. Donald Mercurial restored order to our lives and to community life, I decided it was time to see what Malcolm had been scribbling on his paper and pad day after day. When he wasn't around, I read what he wrote. It was a treasure chest of one man's fantasy life; it revealed his unconscious desires and subconscious motivations. Entries read, "Wouldn't it be great to have a threesome with Martin and Ben," "I feel sad because I can't talk to Ben" and "Can I tell Ben about Martin?" I dropped the clipboard, picked it up, and put it back. I heard footsteps, but they were from downstairs not upstairs, and I took off.

Outside I could smell the roses that Donald Mercurial had worked so hard to cultivate. I remembered seeing him clutching his clippers, then snipping the dead roses, his movements swift, and unemotional. As he moved his hands from between the thorns, yellow, red, white and peach rosebuds fell to the ground. Soon they would become dust. I thought about the St. Louis native T. S. Eliot's poem *Hallow Man*, where he writes,

Here we go round the prickly pear
Prickly pear prickly pear
Here we go round the prickly pear
At five o'clock in the morning.
Between the idea
And the reality
Between the motion
And the act
Falls the Shadow
For Thine is the Kingdom

In time we were always God's, and when time ended, at death, surely ours would be the Kingdom of God. Was it mere coincidence that Eliot's home had an address on Westminster Place?

By the spring Malcolm and Martin were preparing to graduate. I was heading to Kansas City, before heading to the Sacred Heart Retreat House, in Sedalia, Colorado for my eight-day retreat. I needed closure. I needed to tell Malcolm about everything I had read, to confront him, to tell him to get out of religious life before it killed him. Or was I talking about myself?

Just days before my departure, the Bellarmine House of Studies threw its annual year end thank you party. We welcomed all the people we'd worked with in ministry. That year I visited homebound people, shut-ins as they call them in Missouri, and I directed a retreatant on the 19th Annotation format of St. Ignatius' Long Retreat. The 19th Annotation retreat is referred to as *The Spiritual Exercises in Everyday Life*. I decided to make a favorite dish of mine that, thanks to America's chef Martha Stewart, had become well known amongst the Scholastics. As I made it, I thought about Malcolm, and the night we made perogies together, handmade, when he threw flour on me, and held me in the kitchen, before leading me by hand to a guestroom in the First House. He wanted so desperately for me to sleep with him that night. I resisted.

When I was finished, I grabbed a glass of wine and joined my friend Jeff Niles on the porch. Then I saw Malcolm, I looked at Jeff, who looked at me, and I could tell he knew about us, but he never said anything. [If only he had made what he knew explicit, isn't that the discursive commitment?] I wanted Jeff to call Malcolm and me out, to publicly confront us and to tell us that we belonged to the Society of Jesus and not to take it for granted. That simple recognition might have helped change our course, but hindsight is 20/20—even St. Ignatius let a mule direct his course of action when he stood at a crossroads. Rather than kill a Moor for insulting the Blessed Virgin Mary, the mule carried him on toward Jerusalem. That night, I left Jeff and joined Malcolm on the road.

Malcolm and I took a walk toward our usual spot. We passed other sites where we kissed and held each other, like on the very top of the Jesuit Community, a former hotel with an amazing vista of the city. The conversation turned mundane, with my deciding to take charge. Then I asked him if he wanted to have sex with me? He immediately said yes. I said I'll meet you at your bedroom, in the Fourth House. I couldn't believe it.

I met Malcolm at his bedroom door, he invited me in, and we had sex, and two days later we again had sex. (Most gay men would not pass up sex with a guy who referred to his penis as "The Amazon.")

Ironically, I then left for my retreat and for New York City, where I'd live at the Xavier High School Jesuit Community and work at New York Presbyterian Hospital as a social work intern. While in New York City, Malcolm would call my room, leave messages, but mostly he called, early into the morning, telling me he loved me and desiring phone sex. Then, one day I called him back, and we actually spoke. He said it was the decision of the Society of Jesus to send him to a behavioral modification program for sexual addicts. He said he couldn't speak to me anymore, because if he did, they'd dismiss him. And he, like all of us for a time, desperately desired to remain Jesuits.

In many ways, over the next two years I'd find my own flourishing thwarted. Malcolm was still in St. Louis, I'd see him often enough, but he couldn't speak with me. Once, when I was supposed to attend a formation gathering of men in New Orleans, Malcolm drummed up some excuse, telling his superiors that if I went, he could not go. When I hemmed and hawed, and finally told Fr. Donald Mercurial that I would not go, he stormed up the stairs looking for me; from the bathroom I heard him ask my neighbor, Steven Waylay "Where's Ben? I've never been so angry in my entire life." I was filled with anxiety.

We did finally talk about our relationship, that it was existentially confusing, that I was sure I loved him, and that his silence hurt me—I told Mercurial that it was not the kind of love one leaves religious life for, not the type of love that St. Ignatius would encourage a person to take to discernment about the stage and place of one's life. I decided that my love for Malcolm could never be realized because I desired to become a Jesuit priest, but I remained confused about why he was ordered not to speak to me.

Over the next year and a half I made my way back to the center, by focusing on what was most important in my life, to what gave me joy, and to what gave me peace. My affair with Malcolm affected me deeply, not only because of its public nature, but because there was no closure, or forgiveness. Isn't this the same type of mental state most Roman Catholic LGBTQ people find themselves in: at a crossroad between sin and reconciliation. Forgiveness thusly offered to them as the only mechanism for stability in their membership. In due time, I was finishing my studies and working on a framework for the philosophy of human flourishing. My thesis pursued Mohandas K. Gandhi's comments about the well-being of all. He states:

> Man should earnestly desire the well-being of all God's creation and pray that he may have the strength to do so. In desiring the well-being of all lies his own welfare; he who desires only his own or his community's welfare is selfish and it can never be well with him.

What haunted my dreams was the voices of LGBTQ youth so negatively affected by anti-gay theology and anti-gay rhetoric. I remembered my own rejection by my family and by my Church. Not every LGBTQ person can be celibate, nor is every LGBTQ person called to celibacy by God. I desired to confront dogmatism and domination, patriarchy and power.

One night while relaxing on the back porch, Brother Bob Right interrupted a conversation between our new frumpy rector Tommy, my friends and me. He said, I need to speak to you, right now!

Brother Bob Right said that he'd read a draft of my thesis (Human Flourishing) and wanted to tell me, Don't go any further. Not now, not before you are ordained. I asked, Will I ever be able to be gay publicly? He didn't answer my question. He said to write about human flourishing generally and I heeded his advice. (Fr. John Languish censored me before I was a Jesuit, now the Jesuits censored me: I started thinking, did the gay Jesuits I met in New York mislead me about being able to be out, to be able to work directly with and for LGBTQ people in more ways than pastorally, *e.g.*, to confront the Catechism directly through my intellectual writing?)

Brother Right said, I could write about racism and white supremacy, dialogue and democracy, identity and recognition, but not to expect the same tolerance for homophobia and heterosexism. To me it was all the product of social sin, structural evil, something that the free market was dragging its feet to change. I told him why I wanted to write about injustices against the LGBTQ community. Still he persisted in his steering me away from addressing the concerns of the LGBTQ community.

To me, the Church had helped to perpetuate the myth of the "gay person": who, according to the Catechism of the Catholic Church remained intrinsically disordered. The Church gives primacy to Natural Law theory that supports the ends of procreation for every sex act. As such, gay men have two options: voluntary celibacy as a priest or brother, or involuntary celibacy as a single man.

By the end of my conversation with Brother Right, I was drained and sleepy. I said goodnight. Before I went to my bedroom, I looked back towards the porch, where my new rector and friends were. There, I saw the flickering of the candles, felt the cool breeze coming in. I heard Tommy stirring his scotch. I heard his favorite band, the Pink Martinis, singing the song *Mar Desconocido*, written by Martin Zarza,

> Sin mapa ni guia cai en ti
> En tu marea yo me perdi
> Navegar a ciegas esta pasion,
> Barco en las olas de tu Corazon.
> Me pregunte cuando parti
> Si esta corriente llegaba a ti
> Solo quede con mi ilusion
> Isla perdida de una ficcion.

The words of the song are translated this way: [Jesus,] with no map or guide, I fell into you. In your tide I missed, browse my passions blind, my ship on the waves of your heart.

As I drifted off into the night, I asked for the grace that Jesus slumber in me, and that God place me with God's Son, such was the very mystical vision that St. Ignatius had, when he was in La Storta. Like St. Ignatius I longed to follow Christ crucified. And I would, but not to Rome, instead to Saint Peter's Preparatory School in Jersey City, New Jersey. I thought, *Ad Majorem Dei Gloriam*, All for the Greater Glory of God. At heart, I was still very much a Jesuit.

Chapter 9

St. Peter's Horror Show

THE UNITED STATES JESUIT Conference issues the following prescriptions to Regents in a document entitled *Regency as a Stage in Formation*,

> The specific aim of regency is to deepen the spiritual integration and the human maturation of the Jesuit in all its aspects, through serious and responsible commitment to an apostolic activity, with its objective demands of organization, regularity, adequate evaluation of time and means used, of collaboration and service to others. It is expected that this will be effected by challenging the Jesuit in formation to apostolic action in the heart of community where he must learn to live and to contribute his share in a brotherly way to the work of an apostolic team, in which collaboration can be experienced with non-Jesuits, including lay people, and in which the call to serve the Church concretely comes to the forefront.

That sentiment is also contained in another Jesuit document, the *General Norms of Studies of Ours*; both are aimed at knowledge of the men who have asked to become members of the Society of Jesus. Jesuit regents know they are being closely watched and evaluated, but don't resent it because such scrutiny is part and parcel of every religious order. I accepted the fact that the order must somehow deem whether or not I was worthy to become a Jesuit priest and whether or not I was intellectually up to the task of their strenuous formation, involving not only scholarship but engagement with the world through missionary and social work. I clearly understood that by being advanced to Regency by my Provincial, that he had put great trust me, knowing personally about the depth of my desire to be a good and healthy and employable Jesuit.

My provincials knew me well, yearly manifestations of conscience led them to know the depth of my desires and the tangible experiences of consolation, desolation, desert and hope in my prayer. They praised me for my generosity; they praised me for my honesty, validating the fortitude and conviction with which I sought to live out my Jesuit vocation. It was not something they said lightly; in turn, the strengths they reflected back to me enkindled in me a desire to improve my strengths as well gain insight into my weaknesses, all of which was a part of my life's direction: toward priesthood as an openly gay Jesuit in the Roman Catholic Church. I never ran away from my sexuality, no, that was no longer a skeleton in my closet.

Throughout my formation as a Jesuit, my vocation to the priesthood was most important in my life. But there is another added dimension, one I was unprepared for: *It was my sense of belonging to the Society of Jesus, to a company of men who live in solidarity with the poor, who were committed to social justice.* These men had become my family, and because of them, I'd have an identity, and I'd never be lonely, though at times I did feel alone. And as with all families, sometimes I shone bright, knowing well that I had done good work. But sometimes I felt as if I had let them down, and then I would resolve to work harder.

Simply put, I loved being a Jesuit!

The Society of Jesus' General Congregation 32 defined the Jesuit this way: *What is it to be a Jesuit? It is to know that one is a sinner, yet called to be a companion of Jesus as Ignatius was: Ignatius, who begged the Blessed Virgin to "place him with her Son," and who then saw the Father himself ask Jesus, carrying his Cross, to take this pilgrim into his company.* As I left St. Louis for Regency I say again, I was enamored with my life as a Jesuit.

While I don't think of my life as a novel or expose, I sometimes caught elements of magical realism. And I'd sometimes imagined my life as told through the lens of Gabriel García Márquez and Isabel Allende, Latin American authors who'd tell about the meeting of raw life with something like a dream, something far too strange to believe. Which isn't foreign for one living in a religious order, for in such a world one is imbued with a heightened sense of mystery. Thus, one can ask, Is Genesis merely a story? I for sure know that it is far more than that.

When my dad died in 2010, I was learning how to teach in a six-week crash course of study called Jesuit Regents School. I worked at Bellarmine Prep in San Jose, living on the campus of Santa Clara University. The weather was amazing, sunlight, blue skies and warmth. I worked with my classmates on lesson plans and student teaching. None of us had degrees in education, nor had we taught before. The crash course attempted to cram into us teaching's best practices; much of its educational philosophy was taken from a text on Ignatian pedagogy by the Jesuit Ralph Metts, titled *Ignatius Knew*. In a summer whose weather was almost paradise, there was one dark cloud hanging over me: my dad was battling bladder cancer, ever since January. How many times I'd drop to the floor to pray for him. How many rosaries for him. How many Holy Communions offered for him. I loved my dad so much, and more than anything, I wanted him to get well, not only for me but for my siblings and my mom.

In the midst of dark, there is also light. When I met the Jesuit Jerry Blockwood, he was coming home from lessons in sword fighting, carrying a black duffle bag that contained his swords. He looked like a ninja, and when he celebrated mass on Sunday, he exhibited a different kind of stealth. He also made homemade ice cream, which his community spoke highly about during socials. Then there was George Finn, a rather strongly built, Chelsea inspired Jesuit, who wore Zara jeans and Abercrombie and Fitch shirts. When he celebrated mass, the conservative Jesuit Scholastic Van Swift noticeably cringed, with frowns, smiles, smirks and sighs. At community mass Jerry and George sat in the back, or often alone. When it came time for the sign of peace, they were friendly enough; perhaps they were introverts who needed their space.

One week, my peer Sid Songwood got a severe cold, blaming the superior's hypo-allergenic dog Muffin. That week, all he'd say was, "Damn that dog" or "I'm drinking liters of orange juice because of Muffin." We all tried to remind him that the dog couldn't have caused his ailments. When he started feigning illness, with a washcloth on his forehead, I finally said, "Sid, the only way Muffin could've made you sick is if you had French kissed her."

On July 16th, after two-weeks in the hospital, my dad succumbed to his illness. My sister Catharine called me, "Remember, how I'd always tell you the truth about our dad; well, he died—now, come home." My family had kept me at bay, not wanting to disrupt my formation, being hyper vigilant about my becoming a Jesuit priest. Why their concern and scrutiny? That I *not* be actively gay?

Since I felt that my family had no sense of my dad's decline, I started to rage at not being able to visit my dad in the hospital. I had asked my sister to send photos of my dad lying in his hospital bed. Gazing at the photos of my dad in agony, I prayed to Jesus for him, remembering how I prayed with Jesus' passion and death during my Long Retreat. Weeping, I thought about my last real conversation with him on July 4th, when he informed me of his several bad falls, and I told him I was on the beach in California with some close Jesuit friends. We talked about a lot of things; he said, "Always be a good little boy. I love you." I'd always be his little boy. I am proud of it! As my dad declined, his mind went with him; I never spoke to him in the hospital. When I called my mom, I did hear him sputtering nonsense in the background. I encouraged my mom to pray with Psalms 27 and 34. We all needed to trust in God; my dad would be sorely missed. "Al the kiddies pal," as my older cousins referred to him, a pet nickname for their favorite uncle.

After fifty plus years of caring for him, my mom was exhausted. She was ever my dad's bedrock. No doubt about it, she loved and tended to dad, and when I eulogized my dad, I pointed out that without my mom, my dad may well not have been able to be himself. Later, when my mom, Loretta died in September 2019 the local parish priest at Saint Isadore's in Riverhead, N.Y. refused to let me eulogize my mother because he knew of my sexuality and about some of my published writings. Rather than be empathic and allow me to honor our mother he rejected me, a gay man. Somehow my Aunt gave me communion—the look on the priest's face read heartless indignation. What was on his heart? Worse still, the Diocese of Rockville Center suggested in an email that it was my family's decision. Imagine, this is the supposed gay friendly Church of Pope Francis I!

My mom was there for him, and often he was lost. As Jesus took care of his lost sheep, my mom took care of her husband. She was his wife, his lover, his friend, his soul mate, his nurse, his doctor and his priest. Yes, my mom would've been a damn good priest!

When I was what felt like 50,000 feet in the air, flying home, I started to experience symptoms of panic. I felt as if I couldn't be emotional, couldn't cry. I didn't want my seatmates to think I was emotionally disturbed. I did some breathing exercises, and when that didn't work I asked for some Dewar's! Then I just let the tears stream down my face until I passed out.

When I woke up, it hit me: I was an orphan! My dad was gone! I'd never see him again, never hear him, never speak to him, never be with him. A host of "nevers" smacked me, and I wept again. I had thought I had time to solve the enigma of my dad, discover what had caused him to move away from the world, away from us. I'd never really known him, and now he'd always remain a mystery. And I wouldn't have the pleasure of being his friend, on equal foot as adults. No fulfillment there, only sorrow and missed opportunities.

At the time, I was teaching William Golding's *Lord of the Flies* to eighth graders as part of the summer English curriculum, this strange story of boys going a bit mad. My dad had a simpler, gentler view of humankind than Golding, perhaps that is what trauma, addiction and chronic mental health issues afford a person: The ability to be empathetic, to see, whether in thin spaces or not, the promise and beauty of God's beloved children. I kept my copy of the text for a long time; maybe in this classic, I'd find hints as to just who Albert James Brenkert was as a boy. William Wordsworth says, "The child is father to the man." But in the end it was just wishful thinking.

A Jesuit friend gave me Fawn Donaldson's poem, "To Those I Love and Those Who Love Me":

> When I am gone, release me, let me go,
> I have so many things to see and do.
> You mustn't tie yourself to me with tears.
> Be thankful for our beautiful years.
> I gave you my love, you can only guess
> How much you gave in happiness.
> I thank you for the love you each have shown,
> But now it's time I traveled alone.
> So grieve a while for me, if grieve you must,
> Then let your grief be comforted by trust.
> It's only for a time that we must part,
> So bless the memories within your heart.
> I won't be far away, for life goes on,
> And if you need me, call and I will come.
> Though you can't see or touch me, I'll be near,
> And if you listen with your heart, you'll hear
> All my love around you soft and clear,
> And then, when you must come this way alone,
> I'll greet you with a smile and say "Welcome Home"—
> Absent from the body; present with the Lord.

Her poem said what I needed to hear. I've always believed in the power of poetry to help us live our lives.

My Jesuit family rallied around me (and my family), leaving me speechless. Their support and encouragement remains a paradox, for now, as a layman, when I look at my Vow Cross, which hangs on my bedroom wall, I yearn for moments of community like this moment when brother-hood outweighed person, when friendship wasn't transient, before I'd be-come "dead to the Society," when during times of crisis the Suscipe Prayer of St. Ignatius Loyola made most sense:

> Take, Lord, and receive all my liberty, my memory, my understanding, and my entire will, All I have and call my own.
> You have given all to me. To you, Lord, I return it.
> Everything is yours; do with it what you will.
> Give me only your love and your grace, that is enough for me.

What didn't make sense was the reason why my sister Catharine and I had to go to the morgue to identify my dad's body. Had the hospital listed his death as a murder? When the Nassau County employee drew back the curtain, my dad lay, just like in scenes from television's Law and Order or CSI: Miami: On a silver aluminum bed, draped in white, only his head available for us to see. We nodded, "Yes, that's our dad, our loved one, Albert James Brenkert." The employee said thank you, then drew back the curtain. Outside in the waiting room other Latino, African-American and Caucasian families waited for the same gruesome unveiling.

After the funeral and family time, I got ready for the upcoming school year. I prepared lesson after lesson, file after file. I worked at not being emotional. To be honest, I didn't want to teach, especially not religion to sophomores. But it was my assignment, my mission. When I stepped into the classroom, I brought with me my sorrow and my anger; thus, I had trouble forming a good relationship with my students. My first year became the year I was nicknamed "AP Jesus" because I was assigning readings to ninth graders from university professors like Dale Martin, Bart Ehrman, Gerhard Thiessen, the Jesuits Daniel Scholz and Thomas Rausch.

At my first parent teacher night, I had made it through meetings with the parents of my bright and more capable students, but when I entered my last class, it reminded me of Palm Sunday mass with the crowd's shouting, *Crucify him, Crucify him!*

The parents had labeled me as arrogant, said that their children couldn't do the work I assigned. They said, "Our sons hate you," and asked, "What are you trying to prove?" They told me I wasn't ZAP, the beloved living, breathing Jesuit icon who most believed had been at Prep his entire Jesuit life. ZAP fed students hot dogs, never slept and attended every football, soccer, basketball and baseball game, where he incessantly snapped photos with his camera. His office was lined with photographs from floor to wall of students clothed and shirtless, students jumping into pools during retreats and marrying their wives. He was ubiquitous, magnanimous and bespoke charm. Already humbled, I was stunned by the chagrin and disingenuousness of these parents, who naïvely compared me to ZAP. But then, I thought, isn't this what Regency is about?, to find out what I'm good at and not good at, to fail and not to count the cost.

The chaotic high school environment and dysregulated system led me to regress, to negatively cope and to fall apart. I started to overeat, for food had become a source of comforting. And naturally I put on weight. And I started to drink, not looking so much for comfort as a state of forgetfulness. Being the youngest person in my community didn't help matters, for there was no one my age I could talk to. The nearest Jesuit to me in age was close to fifty!

Some nights I'd be at dinner with Brother Erick Surreal, the Jesuit Puppeteer, who talked often about his Ukranian roots and Ukranian dancers. As we ate, I shoveled food into my mouth, while he told me about the girls he coached at the Loyola School. The games he talked about were at times thirty-years old, but he remembered plays, the names of the girls, the scores; he remembered where they were five years ago, and cards they sent him on his birthday. With him, or our ex-chain smoker "bookie," a brother deacon, I couldn't get a word in edge wise. The "bookie" was good for giving me money, money I desperately needed to buy larger pants, larger shirts and alcohol for Fridays after school, where faculty and staff took in rounds of drinks at Captain Al's or O'Connell's.

I couldn't believe how much drink we teachers at Saint Peter's consumed. Is this what teachers did? We worked Monday through Friday only to go out on Friday and drink alcohol! Between buying yourself a drink and rounds for everyone, I watched the register ring higher and higher. I felt capricious, but ultimately drawn to oblige; in doing so, my monthly stipend, then $450, was taxed by returning the favor of drinks to my dominantly Irish cast of educators. Of course, they treated me like an Irish cousin! Like the school itself, our drinking was frenetic, chaotic, some faculty should not have driven home, or they may have sent messages about which they would be embarrassed about the next day.

My friends included Erica Knew, Leila Doubt, Jack Knobbs, and Marla Fiorina. My best friends were my fellow first year teachers Jerry Cranmer, Matt Goodwin and Mike Heschel. We often held "teacher snack time" together, where, in my office, we'd vent about the latest trending faculty complaint, like Jared Hinterland's frustration with sharing a classroom, or Emily Brewster's scoffing at the JUG system; JUG stood for Justice Under God. Emily Brewster was Punky Brewster *en vivo*.

At Prep, the students got away with too much. We'd laugh about teacher mannerisms, like the religion teacher who always came in late, or the Spanish teacher that wore magical, healing stones around her neck, who also practiced tai chi. We all laughed when Matt Goodwin, who looked like Harry Potter (without the scar), deployed a plan to make rumors about us all. Goodwin said, "The kids will spread the rumors, and we'll all hear about them!" Goodwin's plan to gain the students affection backfired, when I orchestrated a rumor that he had a swordfish living in a fish tank in his shared apartment. The fish tank was just big enough for the swordfish to swim, and Goodwin developed a system that forced a current, which kept the fish swimming, thinking it was in the ocean. The Prep kids believed it, and it trended beyond my wildest dreams; there were drawings of swordfish around the school. Goodwin would chide me playfully after a rambunctious student, every now and again, questioned him about his swordfish. Without these friends I wouldn't have survived the horror show contrived by the principal, Jonathan Deadwood. Deadwood's leadership style led me to become personally confused and disoriented about just who I was and what I was doing at Prep. In many ways writing about my experience at Prep is cathartic; whereas, truth and truth-telling is healing.

During my Regency assignment, the Administrative team of Jonathan Deadwood and Mimi Dada were charged with firing Cooper Geoff, a science teacher who had wrestled with students in his underwear during a retreat! Yes, we needed a Comedy and Tragedy mask! My friend Mike Heschel also told me that during an interview they were conducting with a prospective new science teacher, Cooper had asked the interviewee something about "testicles and avocados"!

During my second year of teaching, Jonathan Deadwood and Mimi Dada had to fire Lenora Lenin. She terrorized the school with her maverick style and disdain for all things Jesuit, but that did not get her fired. She was fired because she licked a student on the face during a lesson! *Lenin the Licker* hated Prep, once when our director of faculty formation January Bellicose, whose English accent was thick, ran a workshop, the presenter said, "We are all made of stardust," Lenora said, "This is shit" and stormed off.

January Bellicose was working on a doctorate at Fordham University, the subject of which was anti-oppressive education. She studied philosophers of education, psychologists and sociologists like Paulo Freire, Allan Bloom, John Dewey, Margaret Mead and Jean Piaget; she presented often on the place of LGBTQ students in Jesuit run institutions, crafting rigorous and thoughtful presentations for the Jesuit Secondary Education Association (JSEA). Her work on equity and inclusion, and the talents and creativity of LGBTQ people fell on deaf ears. The JSEA would never confront the United States Conference of Catholic Bishops or issue a public statement of student or employment non-discrimination without suffering the loss of their title as Catholic. How could a school be Jesuit and not Catholic? Many of January's colleagues treated her with disdain, hiding their homophobia in warped comments about her personality. She was the brunt of jokes, when, she could have been sainted for confronting injustice, especially in an atmosphere where gay staff could not come out publicly.

It was about this time that Jonathan Deadwood and my relationship soured. He wanted me to teach like my fellow first year teachers Matt Goodwin and Paul George. He wanted me to cook grades, and make it all about my formation. He was being pressured by the then Jesuit President, Fr. Rufus Rickshaw because he wanted to raise the standards of the school, to get more kids into Ivy Leagues. Rickshaw himself was being pressured by benefactors and by rich, white parents.

What better way to raise standards than to give everyone honor grades!

Saint Peter's had started out as an urban, Jesuit school in 1872 and survived decades of almost closing, debt, even through the high crime days of the 1980s and 1990s, when Jersey City was full of violence. Regardless, Rufus was determined to create a Province gem; and having the support of the Provincial, he even became a Province Consulter.

Truth be told, at the end of my first year, I was exhausted. Students demand so much from their teachers, something that as a layperson, I never fully understood. Simply put, teaching isn't an easy job. At the same time, I worked as the school's clinical social worker, and counseled embittered and entrenched faculty, men and women who loathed the administration, taking many liberties to critique the system from the top down.

For some reason, Mimi Dada assigned me the lower students my second year. Since I still didn't understand differentiated assessment or learning styles, I set out to teach these kids the same way I had. But, AP Jesus was too tough, and these students couldn't make the simplest transitions from one class to the next, especially since Sr. Fanny Donatella had failed them in Chemistry.

Yes, I was overworked, had no boundaries, had turned often to Mike Heschel. How I wanted us to be lovers, but nothing came of our relationship. Mike knew how much I disliked my assignment; often I'd say, "If I left the Jesuits, could we find an apartment?" He just looked at me, saying nothing. My friends Leila Doubt and Matt Goodwin helped to nurse me back to health. Still, Jonathan Deadwood was counting the days to my departure.

After Lenora the Licker was fired, Mike Heschel and I pranked Matt Goodwin one day after school. We went to her office and removed her skeleton named "Bones." We wheeled him into Matt's classroom, propped him up next to the teacher's podium, placed one finger down on the Bible and the other clutching a coffee mug and then high fived each other and left.

The next day, I was summoned to meet with Jonathan Deadwood. He asked me about the skeleton, told me that I had prevented the school from closure with Lenora the Licker since the skeleton was hers. He said shape up, or get out. He said, "You will bring Bones to her, along with the three remaining plastic bins she left." I left his office shaking my head.

True, by this time, there was practically a coup. The faculty were incensed by the bizarre leadership style of Jonathan Deadwood, Mimi Dada, January Bellicose, Jim Melancholic and Rufus Riskshaw. While the school was growing, and becoming far whiter than the original intent of the Jesuit founders, the Province didn't in the least interfere.

It was insane!

When I met with my formation assistant, Todd Firefly, he said, "We know Prep is a surreal place to work in." Yes, it definitely was surreal! When I begged him to be reassigned, he said reassignment wasn't possible, to stick it out, or leave the Jesuits. For the first time, I felt the Society was practicing *cura apostolica* at the expense of *cura personalis*, or care for the work over the care of the person, this is not what the Jesuit Constitutions say!

I liked Todd Firefly a lot; he was very compassionate towards me in the Novitiate, even comforting me one night over cookies and milk while I told him about the homophobia I experienced at the hands of Matt and Kris. Firefly knew how tormented and betrayed I felt by Fr. John Languish.

Communication also got me in trouble. I was almost fired. I, perhaps, had unconsciously been trying to be fired since before I arrived! I was beat down, worn out, exhausted. At times I was imprudent because I felt misunderstood, demoralized and undervalued. When most depressed, I sublimated my inner conflicts, including worries about hyper-vigilance regarding my vow of chastity. I knew something wasn't right, I resumed psychotherapy with my old therapist as part of my new self-care plan. That, along with exercise, and regular visits to a nutritionist helped me feel better and grow my depleted self-esteem. Those afternoons I spent some time doing my Examination of Conscience (Examen Prayer) in Washington Square Park, one of my favorite spots in New York City.

I entered psychotherapy with a goal in mind, to seek treatment for interpersonal conflicts, which I discerned resulted from a lack of insight into the chaotic institution I worked in. I went into treatment because I couldn't be openly gay at my job. Other Jesuits at Prep warned me that I'd "get called in to the Provincial's office." I needed talk therapy to process budding relationships, one with an older gay Jesuit, who taught at one of our universities, and a younger gay Jesuit. Both men were wining and dining me, and in the air were sexual overtures; I was running on empty and needed the supportive therapy to ward off any negative coping or acting out. By this time I had learned that some gay Jesuits seek out to satisfy their carnal appetites as a means to an end. By this time, I had matured in my thinking and rejected such overtures outright. In fact, through therapy I grew the confidence to tell that older Jesuit to leave me alone, and after one forgetful drunken night I stayed away from the younger Jesuit, who told me over and over that he had never fallen in love with a man. How tragic, but again those were his skeletons to wrestles with, not mine. I responded well to treatment, and started to flourish.

Over time I gained greater insight into my psychology through the acquisition of self-control—controlling abusive behaviors, moderating hostile moods, maintaining interpersonally responsible conduct and behavior, gaining insight into my circle of influence and consistency in building upon healthy adult friendships. I was thankful to theorists like Hanz Kohut who taught that "self states" are met when one is in right a relationship with self and others. I even self-administered the Millon Clinical Multiaxial Inventory—III (MCMI-III) during a graduate class at Fordham University. I self-administered this test to grow in the knowledge of the theory, administration, scoring and interpretation of objective instruments used to evaluate personality, emotional adjustment, and attitude toward taking tests. My report earned me an A.

After moving to our community on fourteenth Street, where my new superior was Ethan Quixotic, and my new buddy, the playwright Warren Casual, I at least had physical distance between Prep and me. I couldn't get to the copier at 3 am. Following two surgeries, one for an umbilical hernia that my doctor had found, and the second to repair my chronically dislocating shoulder, I felt even more wiped out. I had to face it, I was in bad shape both physically and psychologically.

All I wanted was to be was a priest!

Then the email I mentioned came: One day, after careful crafting, I emailed parents of three students who, I thought, needed a change of scenery. My mistake: I sent a copy (cc) to every administrator I could, and I hit send.

The next day Jonathan Deadwood called me in, but this time he brought support. With Bones it was he and I, now; he brought in my supervisors, Jim Gluck and Bee Serenade. Deadwood served me papers; he said, "Sign here, you are on probation. You have ninety days to fall in line, or you're out Brenkert."

I was shocked and dejected. I went directly to the chapel and prayed something like this to God: "I'm exhausted Lord, I'm beat up, tired and angry. I love the students and my friends, but this assignment is killing me as well as my vocation. Lord, tell me what to do."

And there was silence. Usually I'd leave chapel with some inspiration, but this time none.

One thing I was sure of: I hadn't heard God's telling me to leave the Jesuits.

I refuse to say I was caught in some dark night of the soul. I won't be that melodramatic, but I wasn't in the light. An inner voice said, Why do you still want to be a Jesuit priest? And another voice countered, It's not about what YOU want, it's about what GOD wants for you.

I recalled the human voices of LGBTQ youth, and thought about the suicide of Rutgers student Tyler Clementi, I thought about the crucifying of Matthew Shepherd, and I thought about the gay students at Prep who had no club. The faces of my fellow gay and lesbian faculty members came to mind, I saw them, some of them with their husbands and wives, some with children. Men and women who couldn't tell their students about their wedding rings, or who had to dissemble or to outright lie.

When I thought about my own ill-treatment by men like Tweedledee and Tweedledum, I begged the Lord, "Let me make it," "Let me work from within, as a priest," "Place me with your son." I couldn't be openly gay because my provincial, formation assistant and rector wouldn't allow it. Fr. Rickshaw often ordered me to stay away from anything controversial, especially any activity with any gay students.

Consequently, I returned to the core of my vocation, to the idea of becoming a gay priest. My spirituality was maturing, and I believed I was following God's will. And I started coaching baseball. I worked with two teams; my first team went undefeated, the second losing some. Both won their championships. I was elated! Baseball was the key. I know, I know, it sounds a bit absurd, but I believe that God sent baseball into my life for a reason, and it's made all the difference. There are no accidents!

I'm no saint, which is now quite clear. During my third year of Regency, I swiped my budget check from my rector's mailbox. Ethan Quixotic didn't find it funny. I raced home from Prep, before class at NYU. I was enrolled in a post-masters program in palliative and end-of-life-care. He said, "Why did you take the check?" I said, "I needed the money." I was put on probation. In truth, I needed help because I was still recovering from my second year at Prep. But mostly, I needed that moment to send me to recovery from alcohol abuse and symptoms of addiction.

I had to face it, I'd been drinking far too much. I had migrated from drinking with my colleagues at work, to drinking alone at home. On Fridays, rather than have a beer or two, I switched to dirty martinis (with olive juice), consuming three or more. The dirtier the better. I was spending money impulsively, and on a few occasions I awkwardly tried to flirt with male friends of coworkers. Once I even drunk-dialed the artist cousin of my coworker, hoping for a tryst later that night.

I started working toward sobriety, learning about my experience, strength and hope, and became blessed with meeting another sober friend, a journalist named Derrick Swift. With Derrick I struggled to stay on the wagon. And little by little, I made it. (God willing, I will have 8 years sober in September 2020.) Ethan Quixotic showed compassion for me, while Warren Casual kept on interjecting his own wisdom and truisms into my life. I loved Ethan and Warren as brothers, but they weren't my dad, and I wasn't their son and I needed my dad but it wasn't God's will for me.

As I reflected on the end of my Regency, I prayed about my next assignment. I'd be moving on to theology, and three years from ordination to the priesthood. The fifteen-year old in me leaped with joy, while the thirty-three year old felt that success and failure was what made voluntary celibacy such a trial. The verdict was neither guilt nor innocence, but rather the procurement of a healthier self, one who could minister to God's people and not cause harm. Other people who practiced sobriety taught me Serenity Now. Even some Jesuits influenced the spirituality of Alcoholics Anonymous.

In my letter requesting permission to move to theology I wrote my provincial:

> Dear Father Provincial,
>
> P.C. Since the 10th grade I have desired to respond to God's invitation to me to become an ordained Catholic priest. Today, some sixteen years later, I write to make a formal request for your approval to continue theology studies in preparation for my ordination to the ministerial priesthood in the Society of Jesus. I have discussed my felt desires to continue with this next phase of formation with my Superior, Fr. Ethan Quixotic and with his encouragement and consent I humbly ask that you consider my request.
>
> The continuity and clarity of my call to the ordained priesthood in the Society of Jesus flows freely from the election I made during the Second Week of the Spiritual Exercises. It is here that I felt God motivating me to freely elect to serve and to praise Him as a Jesuit priest. I also felt consoled knowing that this decision is consonant with my living out God's will for me in my life; to live with God forever. I am consoled because this is what I have desired for most of my life, and I am made humble by discerning that this initiative and calling come directly from God.
>
> My election to petition for theology study in preparation for the ordained priesthood in the Society of Jesus affirms my consciously heard calling first to be a Jesuit: *to know that I am a sinner, yet called to be a companion of Jesus as Ignatius was,* and second to be a Jesuit priest. It is here in the least Society that I am forever to be inspired by the Principle and Foundation and the quest for *Magis.* As a Jesuit priest I am called to be a Christ among God's people. My calling to the priesthood in the Society of Jesus represents a fusion of narratives, where vocation and mission meet in the sending forth of me by my Provincial *in persona Christi.*

The preparatory writing of this petition commenced a period of prayerful discernment through which I looked more deeply into the election I made during my Long Retreat. And it is during this period of prayerful discernment that I (in companionship with Fr. Ethan Quixotic, Fr. Mitch Blessing, my Formation Assistant and Fr. Jorge Cid, my Spiritual Director) have implemented a plan leading to further self-discovery and understanding. This period of discernment led to the clear decision not to apply for a fourth year of Regency but rather to petition to study theology in preparation for the priesthood in the Society of Jesus.

And about my Regency at St. Peter's Prep: I can speak truthfully about a time of personal discovery, about a time of growth and real failure, a time of testing and rebuilding, and a time when through a very recent "bad patch" at Saint Peter's and at home in my community that I further discerned God's calling me to the ordained priesthood in the Society of Jesus.

It is through this most recent process of discernment, where I have worked on some specific issues at school and at home that I have further discerned God's invitation to me to make choices in Christ and to serve God's people as an ordained Jesuit priest. And about this greater clarity, continuity and insight into my vocation, which I have received from this period of prayerful discernment, I can attest that it is faithful, holy, free and virtuous, and also a genuine response to the call of God.

In short, I am deeply consoled about applying for theology study. I feel very free to enter into this new period of discernment, where data about my seven years of Jesuit life and about my living out the vows of poverty, chastity and obedience can confirm my conscious election, and my felt desire to dedicate my entire life as an ordained Catholic priest to the Society of Jesus. Moreover, I am deeply committed to the Society's vision, mission, and prayer for the world; our charism is one that leads to the salvation of souls though our prayers and our apostolates. As our Jesuit brothers write in Decree 2 of General Congregation 35, "Things are no different today. . .the Society seeks to keep the fire of its original inspiration alive in a way that offers warmth and light to our contemporaries. . .we have again and again been privileged to know ourselves as *one* in the Lord: one united, apostolic body seeking what is best for the service of God in the Church and for the world."

Since my entrance to the Novitiate in 2005, I have freely manifested my desires to my Superiors, and accounted for my conscience in annual manifestations with my Provincial, this is in keeping with the mission of the Society: to bear witness to the Gospel. I have done this by performing corporal and spiritual works of mercy to the best of my ability, *e.g.*, as a Novice at St. Peter's Prep, as a retreat director in St. Louis, as a school social worker, guidance counselor, religion teacher and baseball coach during my Regency at St. Peter's Prep, in pastoral and palliative care of my aged brother Jesuits living at Murray-Weigel and throughout my entire Jesuit life as a Jesuit vocation promoter. Through my own actively living out the mission of our least Society, I have been *with Christ at the heart of the world*. And to *go, set the world alight*, I like my Jesuit brothers before me, must maintain a detachment from desires or works that impinge upon my freedom to do the work of God and the Church.

I am enkindled by the promise that my Jesuit priesthood will be dedicated to the total service and love of God and neighbor. I am consoled by the continued loving and generous support of Ethan Quixotic, Mitch Blessing, Jorge Cid, who affirm and support my conscious decision to petition for advancement to theology studies in preparation for my ordination to the priesthood in the Society of Jesus.

Finally, I am freer than ever before to see and to hear God's will for me reflected back to me in prayer, in the face of struggles, smiling friends, dreaming students; in the Sacraments and in and through God's intimacy and initiative with me. For me: Being a Jesuit priest is about making choices in Christ, and for me the Jesuit priesthood in service of God's people fuses with the narratives of other people's lives and experiences along the road.

If my journey to the Jesuit Priesthood is like that of a pilgrim or a companion or a soldier for Christ, then it is only fitting to end my petition for advancement to theology by offering the words of St. Ignatius' *Prayer for Generosity*:

Lord, teach me to be generous.
Teach me to serve you as you deserve;
To give and not to count the cost,
To fight and not to heed the wounds,
To toil and not to seek for rest,
To labor and not to ask for reward,
Save that of knowing that I do your will.

Fraternally yours,
    Benjamin James Brenkert

Chapter 10

Grantland Commons

THE GRACE OF THE Fourth Week of the Spiritual Exercises of St. Ignatius of Loyola is joy. Having already suffered along with Christ through meditation/composition of place, his life and passion, the retreatant fixes his attention upon Easter, upon Christ's conquering death and His resurrection; the retreatant through exquisite attention and fervid faith renders Jesus the core of his/her existence. The Fourth week is the capstone of the retreat, when the retreatant puts on Christ, his *sensus Christi* and sings humbly *Take, Lord, Receive.* If anyone were to ask me about my life, its meaning, its thrust, I would say that Jesus is always, no matter how complicated my life becomes, my *raison d'etre.*

As I left Prep, I was filled with joy; my relationship with Jesus had been confirmed and affirmed in prayer, and my Provincial Dennis Capacious had missioned me to the St. Peter Faber Jesuit Community, located in Boston. I left Prep celebrating the election of Pope Francis I, the first Jesuit Pope in the history of the Roman Catholic Church. It was as if a deadweight, namely the newly minted Pope Emeritus Benedict XVI, had been lifted from the universal church to be replaced with a blast of fresh, invigorating, uplifting air.

I along with 1.2 billion Catholics sighed in relief, imagining a new church, a modern one with both feet not in the twelfth century but in the twenty-first century. A church envisioned by Saint Pope John XXIII, before the curia sabotaged Vatican II. And now we had a pope named after St. Francis; the very name Francis(can) is the antithesis of the elite Jesuits, the saintly founder who heard Christ's call from the cross in Assisi, "Save my church." Yes, I find it ever so ironic, a Jesuit's embracing the poor, lowly, unintellectual Francis, he who dedicated his life to the poor, the marginal, the lepers. This Pope is the pope who laments not eating pizza in the nearby pizzeria, not how long his vestment's train is like Raymond Cardinal Burke (the former Prefect of the Apostolic Signatura).

I was filled with hope.

I also joyed in the historic nature of the Jesuit pope's election. Pope Francis himself had made his way up the ranks of leadership in the Society of Jesus: superior, then Bishop, then Cardinal. The Argentinean Pope, the first non-European Pope, thus made the Jesuits a global subject of interest, if not a trend. People everywhere started wearing shirts, "I heart Jesuits," "Keep Calm and Hire a Jesuit," or "Have a tough job? Hire a Jesuit." Now Jesuit colleges and universities like Georgetown, Wheeling, Le Moyne, Santa Clara, Gonzaga and Spring Hill had universal and unequivocal recognition. Joy is the lens, the hermeneutic through which Pope Francis interpreted the word. Again, Pope Francis by choosing a Franciscan namesake identified with the materially poor, while emphasizing paschal joy; he confronted material or physical poverty; he swiftly challenged the world, "Whose feet will you wash today?"

With Pope Francis it was as if the entire Catholic world were filled with hope and joy, praying Spiritual Exercise 237, praying for all of God's creation to participate in God's universal and cosmological vision, the Beloved Community. In Spiritual Exercise 237 the prayer is instructed, "To see how all that is good and every gift *descends from on high.* Thus, one's limited *power* descends from the supreme and infinite power above—and similarly with *justice,* goodness, pity, mercy, etc.—as *rays* descend *from the sun* and *waters from a fountain."* With Pope Francis I so many hoped, perhaps like Ignatius himself so long ago, the Rules for Thinking with the Church would not call for blind orthodoxy, as Fr. John O'Malley wrote in America Magazine, "we should praise," "we must be careful in speaking," "we should be cautious" - all in an effort "to help people who find themselves in certain situations." And who is in a more difficult situation than the most marginalized members in the Church: LGBTQ people.

During that summer, I'd take my joy and hope with me to Brazil, where I'd participate in the Society of Jesus' MAGIS program for World Youth Day.

Brazil would become the launching pad for Pope Francis; his world stage tour began with a rock concert for youth. Brazil herself benefited from the Pope's visit, one that would be followed by the FIFA World Cup and the Summer Olympics. I learned two things that summer in Brazil: First, Catholic youth from around the world are invested in their faith, their huge presence was proof that the ideology of aggressive atheism and secularism hasn't won. Second, that small, Catholic nuns, throw powerful jabs! I had plenty of welts from nuns tackling me to get as close as they could to Pope Francis. Ouch!

Still, with as much fun and as much joy as I had rocking with my fellow Catholics, or heading to the famous Copacabana Beach to observe the Pope from miles away, there remained an air of mystery about this Pope who allowed hundreds to take selfies of him with adorable children. He dressed simply and plainly. No Prada shoes!

As I left Copacabana Beach, to catch a plane to Sao Paulo, where I'd make my annual eight-day retreat in Spanish, I looked around and watched people furrowing into the sand, getting ready to sleep, all patiently and joyfully awaiting the Papal mass the next day. The Pope would imitate Christ, offering himself to over a hundred thousand of men, women and children, a Eucharist mightily rivaling the multiplication of the loaves or the feeding of the 5,000.

How could anyone doubt Jesus, "I will be with you always?"

When on retreat, I met a Brazilian priest whose Bishop had sent him into great silence. Over dinner we were allowed to chat. I had had a full day's worth of quiet and prayer; I also tried to feed the wild peacocks (to no avail!).

We both were a little restless. With me about to head to theology at the Boston College School of Theology and Ministry. With him to discern whether or not he'd remain a priest. We were two men joined to God in religious life, living vows, and loving others first. And yet, I was preparing to begin my life as a Jesuit priest. While he was to consider whether or not to leave the diocesan priesthood. I had a chance to ask him a thousand questions about what it's like being a priest, but I decided against it. I would let him reveal what he wants, I did not want to intrude upon his silence.

I had already decided not to go to the Jesuit School in Berkeley, California, because Malcolm Boyd was there, and I knew that behavior modification or changes of scenery only work for a time. I was committed to my voluntary vow of celibacy and had been celibate for six and a half years. I would not risk being near Malcolm; I desired priesthood, not another affair.

The Brazilian priest, I was told, was restless because his Bishop thought he no longer was called to the priesthood, since he was being called to be a father, or a husband. The priest told me about the many priests he knew who were both priest and a father or husband, who had secret families; such, he said was also the case in Africa. I could neither verify nor rely on this man's facts. But in his eyes I did see pain, and prayed for him, that he, like Pope Francis, would find, live, and believe in the joy of the Gospel.

As my retreat wrapped up, I headed back to the airport, my retreat director finally speaking English fluently. I was happy to have made my retreat in Spanish; after all, the United States Jesuit Conference wanted every Jesuit to become fluent in Spanish. I joyed in being a Jesuit in good standing. My new formation assistant, Fr. Mitch Blessing, who was a dear friend of Fr. Jerry Conscience, said that by being approved for theology, the Jesuits and the Church were tacitly approving me for ordination.

As I arrived in Boston, the city of Boston Strong, Harvard University, the Charles River, the Red Sox, the Boston Tea Party, the Patriots, I knew that I'd resume psychotherapy, and that I'd continue to work on a fear of proclaiming readings in public. For sometime, I'd simply breakdown while proclaiming the readings; it was certainly performance anxiety. I felt as if the Jesuits around me were judging me, either because they knew of my affairs with Malcolm and Earl, or because they thought, that I, a gay Jesuit, didn't belong in the order.

In Boston, there were many, many of the most hardened, conservative and traditional young Jesuits in the order. Many of whom would not speak to me because they considered me too liberal and too progressive; they knew I worked for Senator Hillary Clinton, that I supported gay marriage, but weren't we all Jesuits, all soldiers for Christ?

The Theologate, as its called, welcomes Jesuits from around the world to pursue degrees in divinity, licenses in sacred theology or masters in theology. Men came from Africa, Europe and Latin America. I felt it was too large a community, some sixty plus men with one rector, Jared Grantland, and his assistant Dan Ruby.

Jared was a thin and anxious sort, a man in his fifties. He was from the Chicago Province. Although a simple man, he had a complex job in caring for so many men, their physical well-being as well as their spiritual and intellectual well-being. A tremendous job for one man! No wonder he jogged as often and as far as he could.

Of course, as always with the church, there is politics. He had to agilely address the growing chasm between what was the Weston Jesuit School of Theology, located in Cambridge, near Harvard Divinity School, and the Episcopal Divinity School as well as the newly burnished Boston College-President funded Boston College School of Theology and Ministry. Three competing theological schools located in Boston, one of our smallest urban centers, with a population of only 700,000 was sure to become a problem.

But make no mistake, what happened at Weston stayed at Weston. Loyalty was the *sine quo non* of being a Jesuit! One older Jesuit said that once that during a party the Jesuits celebrated a mass where, rather than wine, the Jesuit priest consecrated champagne. Apocryphal? I doubt it.

In Boston I lived in a small Jesuit Community with attached townhouses; the site looked like a village of ski lodges, and I quickly took to calling it Grantland Commons. Everything was new: stainless steal appliances, patio furniture, flat screen televisions, wireless internet, fire retardant and resistant furniture. Every Jesuit had his own bathroom, a first for many of us. We didn't even shovel our own snow, or landscape the lawns! Once some conservative Jesuits threw a Kentucky Derby bash, where white people wore colored pants and sipped expensive wine. I looked down from my second floor window, thinking about how far we were from Pope Francis' call to live simply. Jesuit superiors had for a long time tried to get us "to live honestly our slender means," but there is nothing slender about a Kentucky Derby party or the constant flow of expensive wine.

At Grantland Commons, guys would lump together according to interests. I was reunited with Z-Dicks, Jolly, the Bishop, Tyler-no-plain-clothes, Tweedledum and Martin Powder. Jolly still found it easier to be with non-Jesuits, especially women, Z-Dicks still got drunk, the Bishop was still a self-proclaimed saint, who now ran a blog for younger Jesuits. Tyler-no-plain-clothes became even more radical, following the tea party, and feeling "personally wounded" by President Barack Obama's election. Tweedledum evolved; he was more pernicious now, able to masquerade as a leader of the order by day, a womanizer and homophobe at night. Martin Powder still liked choice wine, nice cigars, expensive clothes; he received a trunk of new clothes every month— some he'd keep, others he'd return. We all made it to the finish line. And I did my best to keep up, to follow the call to be a saint! The Jesuit theologian Fr. Stanley Marrow writes, "Sanctification describes not only the saint's static condition but their dynamic vocation. The 'call' to sanctify, like that of Paul's to apostleship, and the call of the church itself, is the effective imperative of the will of God." Thanks be to God! I needed spiritual direction badly.

I met with Fr. Dirk Saccharine, a Jesuit who some said had been a Trappist monk, but who had, during my long retreat figured out Tweedledee and Tweedledum in ways Fr. John Languish never could. After they wheedled him for a cigarette, making some ridiculous comment, Dirk said, "those guys are assholes." I smiled, what do the French say, *plus ça change, plus c'est la même chose*. And Fr. John Languish continued to be blind to their antics, covering their asses all the time. How blind we humans can be at times.

Fr. Saccharine still worked at the Jesuit retreat house in Gloucester, north of Boston and located on the seashore, a beautiful location. I wanted to return, once a month, to this site of my Election to remain in the Society of Jesus and to pursue priestly formation. And I did go every month, each season, and I returned to feeding the swans and gazing at the Atlantic Ocean, whose beauty, power and vastness reminded me that behind all of this was the presence of an agapetic God, one who loves us unconditionally. There before God's grandeur I'd return to Thomas Aquinas' distinctions between apophatic and cataphatic theology, believing God and mystery always won.

In my small community, I was reunited with Jack Broussard, who wouldn't look at me, and I thought he now suffered from a serious case of internalized homophobia. Broussard urgently needed to read Voltaire, Oscar Wilde, or the modern writer Michelangelo Signorile or spend some time volunteering with the Human Rights Campaign or the Harvey Milk Foundation. Instead he got a sun lamp to help him stay happy, and worked long hours as a nurse. Which made me wonder: What are the real options for gay seminarians or gay priests? Even though some of my peers would likely never accept me as a gay, there was one good thing: by year nine in the Society of Jesus it was increasingly clear, once you're in with the Jesuits, you are in, there is no coming out. It was a special kind of club, with permanent membership. Fr. John Languish was right: while heterosexual Jesuits could make crass, sexist jokes about women, or deride ex-girlfriends or ex-fiancés, one was a Jesuit, but never a gay Jesuit. (I do remember going on one summer vacation with three older gay Jesuits, we stayed at the Cazenovia Villa. By then, some younger gay Jesuit friends of mine had left the order, which made choosing a summer vacation spot hard. While this time with my gay Jesuit peers was helpful and completely healthy, e.g., to be amongst other gay Jesuits it all seemed too contrived and forced.)

As I commenced Freudian psychotherapy with my analyst Derrick Jonah, I mixed in with Boston's booming sobriety circuit, class, spiritual direction, mass, community dinner, and ministry, I also worked in my specialty field: palliative and end-of-life care with aged and aging Jesuits. I spent some of my best moments speaking with the great Jesuit theologian, Fr. Dan Harrington—he told me on more than one occasion that my future professor Elisabeth Schussler Fiorenza was universally admired and respected as [a Feminist] theologian. I felt more and more at home. I was settling in, life was good. For a time it was all serene, idyllic, I studied during the day, worked out when I could, prayed and read novels by Colm Toibin, Norman Mailer, Reza Aslan and C.S. Lewis at night. I cooked fun meals like fried polenta, veal and linguine, or perogies, caramelized onions, and kielbasa.

Then to my shock, I was hearing negative comments about Pope Francis. My Fundamental Theology teacher, Kek Abhorrent said the media got him wrong, and far worse, that the Pope was making a buffoonery of the Church. To Kek Abhorrent one could be Catholic only by following and never questioning the Church's catechism, doctrine, dogma, and tradition. He said revelation was closed, the deposit of faith full for all time. Today, Kek Abhorrent has a new audience of like minded traditionalists at Notre Dame University.

I knew Kek Abhorrent was speaking nonsense, but I had no power to contradict him; he was a bully who entertained his admirers through his bully pulpit.

Kek Abhorrent felt wounded, lamenting that Pope Emeritus Benedict XVI had not completely collapsed Vatican II so that we all could return to the good old days. He made it clear, in his newly converted, hostile fashion, that if you didn't agree with the Church, get out. Of course, it was his church! To him, there was one conductor who measured meter, timbre and stanza. And that conductor wasn't the present pope—it was tradition. When I complained to my budding friend, another gay Jesuit, he said to suck it up, as he's got tenure. Ironically, many gay Jesuits completed their theses under his direction. What do they say: *the devil you know is better than the devil you don't know.*

Kek Abhorrent saw my chagrin. He might have seen my disdain. He surely saw my dislike. Kek failed me with the lowest grade I'd ever received in graduate school, a B-.

Yet, Kek was a highly effective orator; of course he was, as he was an alum of Boston College! For a time I almost believed him. The power of conditioning! I started to believe that in my lifetime the Church wouldn't change, she would never ordain women, never allow priests to marry or divorced Catholics to remarry or to receive Holy Communion (more on my naïveté, later).

As he poured forth his nonsense, a worldwide phenomenon occurred, called the Francis Effect: Pope Francis was becoming the most admired and loved religious figure in the world, for his wisdom, his modernity, his love of the poor. And about gays, he said, "Who am I to judge?" Is that not what every gay person in the world wanted to hear? I loved this man! No, Pope Francis could never pass Abhorrent's litmus test. If he had his way, he'd be shunned and banished to Avignon. The sad truth is this: I was shocked that such a man as Abhorrent existed at a Jesuit College, as he so much contradicted everything the Association of Jesuit Colleges and Universities stood for, everything that we teachers at Jesuit Secondary Education Association schools taught our students to avoid. I am thankful that my order also produced men like Francis, Pedro Arrupe, Walter Ciszek, Matteo Ricci, Daniel Berrigan, though in America those men are becoming fewer and fewer.

Then at Harvard, I took a class with Elisabeth Schussler Fiorenza, the theologian who termed the phrase Kyriarchy (oppressive society). One day when I praised Pope Francis, she cut me off, "Before Ben continues, who cares about what Pope Francis is saying?"

I was shocked, turning beet red from embarrassment. Was my Jesuit world so privileged, so white, so arrogant? Had I missed something these past nine years? Or was this just the well-known arrogance of Harvard? Or its arrogant professors? Soon I'd work with her at the *Journal for Feminist Studies in Religion*. There I'd see the contributions of women to the academic discourse on God's Beloved Community.

No one could disabuse me, however, of my love of Pope Francis I.

In Boston, I started to meet more and more sober men and women, including sober gay men. One of the most common themes from their stories centers around death and resurrection. How many of us had come close to death from booze? How many of us had to be reborn into a life without alcohol? Reborn into a new, positive way of thinking and living? And hearing about rebirth and resurrection from men and women who were always fighting to stay sober was a constant inspiration to me. At each meeting I thought of the puzzling, enigmatic figure of Nicodemus, from the Gospel of John. The American theologian Raymond Brown writes that, Nicodemus shows, "How some who were attracted to Jesus did not immediately understand him. Presumably some never came to understand him, but some like Nicodemus did, making his faith public at the burial of Jesus with Joseph of Arimathea."

Wasn't this a simple message, stop drinking and think clearly? In their presence, I felt humbled and accepted.

I found profound community there, with people who wanted to help each other stay sober, with people willing to share their own personal stories of strength, hope and repair. There I could be Ben, the chaste, gay Jesuit, with no judgment, no derision for being out or in the closet; what mattered was staying sober. I started praying with all of this in mind—that is, the suffering of my fellow non-drinking friends. Rather, let me say my non-drinking family. It was the Quaker Emmett Fox who wrote, "The art of life is to live in the present moment and to make that moment as perfect as we can by the realization that we are the instruments and expression of God himself."

In sobriety, I lived each moment as it was, like a golfer plays the ball from where it lies. Over time, I met and befriended a group of sober gay men, going to burger joints after meetings, where we ate salty fries, or Mexican places where we snacked on nachos, helping us form a community of gay sober men.

As gay men are pushed out of Chelsea and the West Village, they await more than full marriage equality, but that's the coercive force of the free market. It is society at large that still rejects gay men, who would rather see them take drugs, party hard, have unprotected sex and die. This society rejects the blood of gay men as unclean, still we cannot donate life saving blood in the United States. A society, that sees itself, at times, through a

Biblical and puritanical lens, (even though its a myth that the founding fathers intended America to be Christian) one that purports traditional marriage, when many of the Bible's very own patriarchs had diverse families and multiple wives.

After meetings, I always returned to Grantland Commons, where I'd rejoin my community that included a Chilean Jesuit I was attracted to; he himself was being delayed and delayed for ordination for his own interpersonal conflicts. I also met with a Turkish Jesuit priest who served at a mass with Pope Emeritus Benedict XVI; he was a Muslim convert. I started watching the Premier League and rooting for Chelsea, who can resist Fernando Torres, Neymar and Oscar. With Richard Season, a Jesuit nicknamed "the silver fox," I talked about the British diver Tom Daley and his budding romance with Dustin Lance Black, while Season told me about his mentorship with Walter Cardinal Kasper, and how the Society once celebrated him for being a Karl Rahner scholar. (Had Cardinal Kasper ever met a gay person?; would he say yes publicly?) Such is the amazing thing about being a Jesuit—one meets people from every kind of background imaginable.

My life had settled into a pattern. I was where I wanted to be, doing what I wanted to do, and looking forward to becoming a Jesuit priest. I was a lucky guy with a full life ahead of me, filled with good work, good friends, and good aspirations. I aspired to the Beatitudes and to complete the Corporal and Spiritual Works of Mercy, to practice the ethics of the Good Samaritan in all my affairs. In short, I wanted to be a good, holy Jesuit priest.

Then out of the blue, I heard about the Church's firing of lesbian and gay employees and volunteers. At first, I couldn't believe it, but the more I thought about it, giving it my complete attention, I realized that it was a lost cause: The Church will not accept homosexuality, bisexuality or transgenders. My church is me. What I represent had rejected gays. I am gay. Thus I am rejected. And if I am rejected because I'm gay, then I can no longer be part of this Church. These were my thoughts at the time of the cruel firings. And afterwards, I became depressed. My bright future suddenly turned dark.

As I upped my meetings with sober friends and started going to psychotherapy three times a week, I thought: Why would the Church fire people of goodwill, who taught the faith to children, who ran food pantries or directed choirs, or who worked in grief and bereavement ministry, or who donated their time, talent and treasure? (Upon further reflection, I could now apply some of the thinking of the American philosopher Judith Butler from her text *The Force of Nonviolence*, suggesting that Mother Church did not mourn, bereave or grieve the loss of these fired employees; Mother

Church severed her ties with the LGBTQ other, thus further negating their value and potential for stewardship moving forward.)

I started to feel personally betrayed. I, who discerned for so long to become a priest, to freely deny myself family, husband, children, and in order to be a gay priest. What was I doing? I thought about my friends who said, in 2004, when my discernment with the Jesuits was just starting, "Why are you are becoming a priest in a Church that rejects gays?" They added, "If the Church loves gays, it's only celibate gays because when gays love, the Church says they are committing serious sin." I had been forewarned.

Nevertheless, I seethed inside. I had no one to talk to about my disappointment, my anger, my feeling of being betrayed by the church I had loved all my life. I didn't want to turn to older gay Jesuits, of which there are many in Boston. These gay Jesuits were past their prime—they either simply did what they wanted, like host private masses with fringe communities, or turned to the arts, as there's no better way to escape reality than by tuning to the music of Verdi, Wagner, Rossini or Puccini. Simultaneously it wasn't a hard question or an unbearable presumption: I could find a way to enjoy my life as a Jesuit even more, despite my protestations on behalf of the vows of poverty; that embedded itself thanks to the classics and Aristotle within Catholicism and linked it to scholasticism and Greek philosophy, the domain of homosexual men. I mean, the Jesuits are the elite.

Thus, I relied on my sober friends and our community, and to good friends from Marist College, including Lea Andrews. I began to speak about leaving the Jesuits, and in the meantime I attended mass at the Episcopal Church. I went to St. Paul's in Brookline, Massachusetts, where I met Father Jacob Miller—he was a stud, married with an adopted Latino son. In this Church priesthood and marriage weren't mutually exclusive, and women priests were called "Mother," not "Father."

I wasn't naïve to think the Episcopal Church was perfect. But she did have gay priests, gay married priests, women priests, priests with children. In the Episcopal Church one could fall in love, and be loved, experience touch, wake up in the middle of the night with a spouse or boyfriend next to them. But those changes came with time, reformation, counterreformation, re-formation. At this point I wanted to belong to a Church that didn't fire people from jobs because of their sexuality or gender identity.

Then I learned about the firing of Colleen Simon and Nicholas Coppola from Jesuit apostolates. I couldn't believe it—what were the pastors of our churches in Kansas City and Oceanside thinking? I filled with sadness when I thought about the tremendous chasm between Bishop William "Mansion" Murphy, Bishop Robert Finn, and Pope Francis. The Jesuits, who had ordained thousands of gay men, fired Simon and Coppola because of their sexuality, because they were married to someone of the same gender. I was incensed. I was weary of the Church's treatment of LGBTQ people.

Of course I knew about the Church's treatment of gays from my adolescence, and through my life in the Jesuit order (to this day). Why enter the Jesuits? Why try to speak truth to power? Perhaps I was too naïve: thinking that by becoming a healthy, generative and openly gay priest my good example could overcome the centuries of homophobic treatment of LGBTQ people. To me it was worth the try because I did not want to devalue or negate the many thousands of good pastoral works performed by closeted gay priests before me.

And my new hero, Pope Francis, was he condoning this treatment of gays? I now had doubts about him. Had he really meant it when he said, "Who am I to judge?" Was he just telling the world through the media what they wanted to hear? As for me, did he really approve of me, and of my desire to become a priest? Will he come out and invite gay people to enter religious life? In short, could I trust him? What about the married gay and lesbian employees at St. Peter's Prep? How secure and safe were their jobs? How many others went to work not knowing if their boss would call them in to say, "You're fired." Was the Church more ruthless than Donald Trump?

Abraham Joshua Heschel, the twentieth century Jewish scholar, activist and theologian, writes that for the prophet a single act of injustice is a disaster for "the prophet is one who feels fiercely." It is the prophet, who according to Heschel, faces God and man through his consciousness, his urging, alarming and facing forward in the face of calamity, catastrophe and chaos. It is Heschel who reminds us that: "What we are depends on what the Sabbath is to us." I heard the "scream" of the prophet, especially when considering the continued violence perpetuated against the LGBTQ community in the United States of America, and the anti-gay legislation codified in countries like Uganda, Russia, Jamaica, Egypt and the Middle East. All the while the Society of Jesus and the United States Conference of Catholic Bishops did nothing.

Feeling hurt, alienated and rejected, I began to attend the Episcopal services on Sundays rather than the Catholic mass. I still went to mass in my community, but I felt so distant. When I looked around or gazed at the Virgin Mary statue that replicated the one St. Ignatius prayed to at Montserrat, where he laid down his sword and sought the Lord, I decided to lay down my sword, to stop fighting for something that would eat at my soul. I had to face the fact that in my lifetime the Church might never recognize or accept the LGBTQ community as full members of the Church. And I was saddened and depressed by this realization. I had actually believed that the negative description of gay people found in the Catechism of the Roman Catholic Church would eventually be erased.

I now discerned that God was calling me *from* the Jesuits.

I made my decision to leave the Jesuits (in 2014) during the Easter Vigil Mass at St. Ignatius Loyola Church, which is located at the end of the Boston College Campus. I had spent some of the Triduum at Episcopal churches, like Trinity in Copley Square, and St. Paul's in Brookline.

The pastor at St. Ignatius Loyola and my friend, Fr. Brent Van Spyke said it was his best liturgy all year, with pageantry, drama and prayer. In addition, there would be several families received into the Church, fulfilling their Baptismal promises. I said yes, and off I went with some members of my small Jesuit community, named after the Jesuit Saint Miguel Pro.

There, at the mass, were two same-sex couples with children—one lesbian, the other gay. When Fr. Brent introduced the catechumens, he said: "Let me introduce tonight's families, we have Mary and Martha, and their child Tony, and Lazarus and John, and their children Seamus and Sean." He said this not once, but whenever such liberties arose in the liturgy. Was repeating the names an act of social justice? The more he repeated their names, and identified the couple as same-sex, the more uncomfortable I felt. With every repetition of their names, I felt almost breathless. The more he pleaded with his congregation to hear "to whom" these children belonged, to the gay and lesbian couple, the more I felt like a fraud.

To me, Fr. Brent was pleading for them to be accepted, to be admitted, to be part of the full community of faith. Why was Fr. Brent "outing" this couple when society sees outing as a negative betrayal of someone's deepest, personal identity, or had they given him permission to do so? Is coming out still a stigma? And does it still endanger a person or person's future in work, friendship, family and faith? What are the reasons why someone might be outed as gay, lesbian, bisexual or transgender? Is there a moral imperative to out people today? (How will the Jesuits receive my memoir, will they look to slander me, and call me "a Judas" or far worse, be silent?) Part of the problem of the Church is that much of its charm reflects its unchanging nature with all its prejudices.

Then it hit me: these children's Baptism was theirs, and theirs only. It was they who would now be received into the Church, and they whom Christ would now adopt. In the sacrament of Baptism what matters is the salvation of souls, not the status of the children's parents as married or un-married. The Church is not concerned about the parents, she is concerned about saving souls. On this point Martin Luther was right, writing in his large catechism in 1529, "To put it most simply, the power, effect, benefit, fruit and purpose of baptism is to save."

Fr. Brent could've said the name of those same-sex couples 10,000 times, but that night the Church celebrated the welcome and baptism of children, *not* the sacramental, life-giving, nature of same-sex families. No, that night, in that rite, the chief claim was ownership in Christ—what the Church and the community of faith present, had done, along with her ambiguity and ambivalence; she, Mother Church, was not being gay-affirming or pro-gay, at a simple, small, service within a Jesuit privileged church. No, this was not liberation, it was false hope!

I thought of the man whom Jesus loved, John the Beloved disciple, the only person in the entire Christian Scripture to lay his head on Jesus' breast. Even the men on the road to Emmaus didn't get that close. As Abraham Joshua Heschel reminds us,

> To believe in God is to fight for God, to fight whatever is against God within ourselves, including our interests when they collide with God's will. Only when, forgetting the ego, we begin to love God, God becomes our need, interest and concern. But the way to love leads through fear lest we transgress God's unconditional command, lest we forget God's need for humanity's righteousness.

I went forward to communion, with resurrection and rebirth on my mind; my eyes welled with tears, but I felt serene. God now confirmed my discernment. It was time for me to rise, and step out into the light.

I, with God's grace, had discerned now to make public my exodus from the Jesuits. I wouldn't idly and passively watch as more and more LGBTQ people were fired and humiliated. I believed, and still do, that God had enkindled in me a gay liberationist theology, that my life would be devoted to helping gays be accepted and loved, but my efforts had more of a chance outside the Catholic church. I felt as if God were speaking to me, "Go, do likewise."

I made my desires known, beginning with my superiors, U.S. Jesuit conference officials, to do something to stop the firing of lesbian and gay employees. I spoke about the tenuous employment of countless married gay and lesbian employees in Jesuit high schools across the country, good men and women who earn a living by modeling/following the tenets of Ignatian spirituality and the charism of St. Ignatius of Loyola. I begged my superiors to work to hire back those that had been let go.

I argued that their losing their jobs and health care, as a consequence of their being found out to be gay or lesbian, had brought them closer to the material poverty that Pope Francis supposedly denounces. I also begged my superiors to help save my vocation by standing firmly not timidly with

LGBTQ people, but they didn't reach out to me, as I had hoped they would. To my dismay, they said, "Ben, this is not a prison, we cannot keep you." These words were said to me by men who were mostly gay themselves, privileged in their own priesthood, others disowned me, but for whom I remained a Jesuit in good standing, and not someone they wanted to see go.

Some Jesuit friends told me to focus on the materially poor, including Latinos. I did not find their distinction between the corporal and spiritual works of mercy valid or licit. Catholic social teaching did not say to privilege the materially poor at the expense of the spiritually lame or disabled or rejected. No, it is Catholic social teaching that calls us to virtue ethics, to build a just society centered on the holiness of the life and dignity of the human person, call to family, community and participation, solidarity and care for God's creation. I would not be timid in my decision, as that was not *Magis*.

In my heart of hearts, I believed that St. Ignatius himself wouldn't have rejected me. He would've done all he could to keep me in his order, as an openly gay, and voluntarily celibate priest! Consider the friendship between Saint Ignatius Loyola and Saint Francis Xavier, Francis who once wrote Ignatius so intimately, "Among many other holy words and consolations of your letter, I read the concluding ones, 'Entirely yours, without power or possibility of ever forgetting you, Ignatio.' I read them with tears, and with tears now write them . . . You tell me how greatly you desire to see me before this life closes. God knows the profound impression that those words of great love made on my soul."

I wish that gay priests would out themselves, but that's a decision each person must make on his own or is it? Moreover, how many more LGBTQ youth might be bullied or may die before these priests come out? Is that a fair question, is the world ever really fair? The gay person can stand before the mirror, like I did, and say, "to be gay is to be beautiful." I would encourage gay priests to come out, though I stand in a small minority who believes outing fully reveals God's beloved creature to the world, and I'd say it requires a lot of courage. Hiding behind one's vow of obedience is cowardly. Jesus never hid.

Many will disagree, but I would say that by not coming out, these gay priests are missing an opportunity to be Christ like, and to help people hear the message of God's love. For what is needed in our world most is agapetic love, a love that creates the Beloved Community. Agapetic love is a love that accepts each person for who he or she is unconditionally. Saying something is pro-Gay, or gay friendly or gay affirmative is more of what the author Ray Bradbury calls "vanilla tapioca" or "the paste pudding norm." When is the Christian ideal of neighborliness ever easy?

Of course, my desire to fight for the rights of LGBTQ Catholics seemed too lite of a reason for my dismissal. I kept on being asked, whether there is anything else or another issue? Other closeted gay Jesuits told me that my departure negated their work, that I was full of hubris, that in staying I could help them. Fr. Grantland and Fr. Blessing asked me to stay, to discern even longer, to pray more; they even offered to delay my ordination so I could be even freer to discern. I was a Jesuit in good standing; they said—take more time.

I went back to the Spiritual Exercises of St. Ignatius Loyola. I prayed Spiritual Exercise 146:

> To consider *the speech* which Christ our Lord delivers to his servants and his friends as he sends them out on this enterprise. He commends them to seek to help all men and women, by attracting them, first, to the high *spiritual poverty*; and if his Divine Majesty be thereby served and should be pleased to choose them for it, not less to *actual poverty*; and secondly, to the desire for *humiliation* and *contempt*. For from these two things follows humility. Therefore, there are these three steps, first, poverty opposed to riches, second, humiliation or contempt as opposed to worldly honor, and thirdly *humility* as opposed to pride. From these three steps they can lead everyone to all other virtues.

I chose God-centeredness over the privilege of the elite Jesuit priesthood. I chose poverty over a life as a Jesuit. I chose to represent, the Jesuit way, the desire for authentic mission, vision and prayer—and I chose to fight for the LGBTQ youth who will likely never meet a Jesuit in their lifetime, but whose diocesan priest tells them they are intrinsically disordered (as is written in the Catholic Catechism).

With sadness I left the Society of Jesus, known as the Jesuit order.

With sadness, I recall, Pope Francis' "Who am I to judge?"

I penned an Open Letter to Pope Francis: Help Save My Vocation. He never called, he never wrote, the Jesuit Curia (the headquarters of the Society of Jesus in Rome) is so close to the Vatican.

I wonder, will he ever say, *I love the LGBTQ community?*

Chapter 11

Sent To the Frontiers

A Jesuit Missioned to the Laity

MY FAVORITE DOCUMENT FROM the Society of Jesus' General Congregation 35 is Decree 3, *Challenges to Our Mission Today: Sent to the Frontiers*. In it, the Jesuits in attendance sought to describe what it means to be a Jesuit on mission in a globalizing, pluralistic and environmentally endangered world. It is, to me, the richest and most intellectual document produced by Jesuits from around the globe. In the document the Jesuits affirm:

> The aim of our mission received from Christ, as presented in the Formula of the Institute, is the service of faith. The integrating principle of our mission is the inseparable link between faith and the promotion of the justice of the Kingdom.
> Thus, the aim of our mission (the service of faith) and its integrating principle (faith directed toward the justice of the Kingdom) are dynamically related to the inculturated proclamation of the Gospel and dialogue with other religious traditions as integral dimensions of evangelization.

It was Pope Emeritus Benedict XVI who told the Jesuits:

> Today I want to encourage you and your brothers to go on in the fulfillment of your mission, in full fidelity to your original charism, in the ecclesial and social context that characterizes the beginning of this millennium. As my predecessors have often

told you, the Church needs you, counts on you, and continues
to turn to you with confidence.

Your Congregation Thirty Five takes place in a period of
great social, economic, and political changes; sharp ethical,
cultural and environmental problems, conflicts of all kinds, but
also of more intense communication among peoples, of new
possibilities of acquaintance and dialogue, of a deep longing
for peace. All these are situations that challenge the Catholic
Church and its ability to announce to our contemporaries the
Word of hope and salvation.

Pope Emeritus Benedict XVI and the Society of Jesus had it right, as
the world is in need of right relationships, with God, self and others. Such
rightness or balance of relationships is becoming of the human good, for
all people are good in themselves because they are created by God. But of
course not all are people equal because some, like LGBTQ people are re-di-
rected away from their human flourishing by churches like Roman Catholicism, e.g., which tells LGBTQ people overtly or through misdirection to
deny themselves the fullness of their character. Ours is a world that longs for
reconciliation—a world that beckons each other *to find God in all things*. A
world charged by Christ to preserve the the life of the other, not to dissemble
one's true teachings with a smile. Hence, the Jesuit Fathers at General Congregation Thirty Five said, that the Jesuits must give *The Spiritual Exercises*,
"to allow the Creator to deal immediately with the creature and the creature
with its Creator and Lord to lead people to a deeper relationship with God
in Christ and through that relationship to service of his Kingdom."

As I packed up my belongings at the St. Peter Faber Jesuit Community
in Boston, I longed to remain a Jesuit. I knew that some of my brothers
thought I was being impetuous. Far worse, I felt they thought my discernment, while spiritual and holy, lacked intellectual rigor, as if discernment
is an algorithm, theorem or hypothesis to prove. Once my rental car was
packed, I sat behind the wheel for a moment and took my final look on the
place I called my last Jesuit home. Next to me sat my Vow Cross, ahead of
me my new Jesuit mission: I had been missioned by the Society of Jesus to
become a layperson (again).

The drive from Boston to Riverdale, in the Bronx, where I'd stay with
an ex-Roman Catholic nun, took about five hours. It was a lot of time, much
of which I spent in silence, thinking about my family that rejected my decision, thinking my being a Jesuit was what God wanted most for me in my
life. Of that, perhaps I could agree. No, I did not enter religious life to save
my soul, no matter how much my Church tried to tell me that gay men have
few options, either choose the voluntary celibacy of the priesthood or the

mandatory celibacy of single life. Yes, the reasons why I left religious life are more endemic to the human condition.

To my very Catholic family, I had made a hasty decision. They clung to my status, even calling the Province office to tell the Province Vocation Director that I'd had a breakdown, or had been terribly misled. To my very Catholic family, deciding to leave religious life to support the LGBTQ community made little sense.

Intellectually I grounded my departure in the rational and logical extension of Feminism, the Ethics of Care. The feminist Nel Noddings writes about the Ethics of Care this way,

> Recognizing that ethical caring requires an effort that is not needed in natural caring does not commit us to a position that elevates ethical caring over natural caring. Immanuel Kant identified the ethical with that which is done out of duty and not out of love, and that distinction in itself seems right. But an ethic built on caring strives to maintain the caring attitude and is thus dependent upon, and not superior to, natural caring. The source of ethical behavior is, then, in twin sentiments— one that feels directly for an other and one that feels for another with that best self, who may accept and sustain the initial feeling rather than reject it.

To those who found Feminism bemusing, I posited a logical or rational extension of the Ethic of the Good Samaritan. The Church, no matter how much *progress* Pope Francis is channeling, remains stuck on sex. I refused to remain a Jesuit, and be silenced by the Roman Curia, like some of my Jesuit brothers.

As I departed, faithful to my vow of obedience, I argued that the LGBTQ community remains comprised of fringe characters and safe outsiders. When the Jesuits missioned me back to the laity, because they would not rehire fired workers like Colleen Simon and Nicholas Coppola, they proved everything I knew to be socially sinful about workplace discrimination. The younger Jesuits I met, besmirched the moral higher ground I sought on this issue; they wantonly redirected me to consider the poverty of refugees, migrants, inner city Black youth, upper class white students who need an education or go to the frontiers of boundary-less nations, to give water to the earth so that food might be produced. To them the LGBTQ weren't poor or fragile enough—they didn't meet the poverty line, for to them, the LGBTQ community could hide or pass, while "the real poor" couldn't.

I cannot see a difference between doctrine and practice. As Cardinal Ratzinger, Pope Emeritus Benedict XVI once wrote,

Doctrine helps create a unity within pluralism; it is faith that signifies an ultimate bond to God, who is truth, it does indeed furnish man with norms for his concrete action in society, yet, the community of believers does not find its center of unity in social or political praxis but only in the authentic binding force of truth itself.

For men and women like Pope Emeritus Benedict XVI, pluralism is a major problem. For such people, it is doctrine then that helps the faithful to distinguish between Truth and truth, Theology and theologies. Hence faith, scripture and doctrine open man to true knowledge, to the truth of his being in God, to know precisely what the dignity of man is in relationship to God's revelation. The revelation of Jesus Christ as Word-made-Flesh, Jesus who loves us and calls us to conversion and to kenosis, is then the theosobia, the incarnated and sacred mystery of our worshipful wonder, the plain and simple teaching at the heart of doctrine, dogma, and tradition.

Doesn't whitewashing the Truth disavow men and women of the ability to distinguish between what the Church Stands For, and what the Church stands for? With mere messaging, repackaging and tonal shifts, the Church denies her very members the capacity and freedom to discern membership, thereby confirming what Karl Marx said, that "religion is the opiate for the masses."

Why be a Jesuit sent to the frontiers if scripture's application to the twenty-first century isn't different from the time of Saints Augustine, Anselm, Benedict, or Bonaventure? In other words, is Pope Francis really changing the Church, as the Boston Globe's reporter John Allen, Jr. suggests, "without altering a single comma in the catechism?" Will Francis outlive the Catechism, or Holy Mother Church? Or is Pope Francis saying that the deposit of faith is settled, that revelation is closed, thus, implicitly agreeing with Pope Emeritus Benedict XVI, though less creedal, and more picturesque or publicly adorable?

The proof to me is in how Saint John Paul II and Pope Emeritus Benedict XVI walked mightily backward the reforms of Vatican II, e.g., slowing the reforms of collegiality and priestly accountability and transparency. Vatican II almost gave women the right to use contraception, and introduced the vernacular in the liturgy. Now, even under Pope Francis, women have such a little place, and the liturgy is increasingly said in Latin (the sacred language), while the translation of the liturgy leans heavily toward formal equivalence (literally word for word).

Thomas Cranmer wrote in his *Defence* (sic Apologia):

> Many corrupt weeds be plucked up. . .But what availeth it to take
> away beeds, pardons, pilgrimages and such other like popery, so
> long as two chief roots remain unpulled up?. . .the very body of
> the tree, or rather the roots of the weeds, is the popish doctrine
> of transubstantiation, of the real presence of Christ's flesh and
> blood in the sacrament of the altar (as they call it), and of the
> sacrifice and oblation of Christ made by the priest for the salva-
> tion of the quick and the dead. Which roots, if they be suffered
> to grow in the Lord's vineyard, they will spread all the ground
> again with the old errors and superstition.

While Pope Francis I has a moral imperative to bring the Church out of Plato's caves and away from Aristotle's forms, to meet the secular and religious and spiritual issues of today, and the future, the Pope Francis Effect has yet to be fully recognized. Is he making the Church stand for those things of the world that need most attention? Only history will judge. Is Pope Francis a social justice pope more interested in confronting realities, like material poverty, than elevating the Church to the spiritual? Only his bishops and priests will demonstrate it. Is Pope Francis revolutionary in his transformation of the Church? Only time will tell. We must be prudent in how we embrace Pope Francis in the short term, for though the Kingdom of God is to come, hence metanoia, the Kingdom of God is already amongst us, in the form of Christ transforming cultures.

As I transitioned from a Jesuit in good standing to lay life, I quickly landed a job at St. Luke's in the Fields, an Episcopal Church located on Hudson Street in New York City. St. Luke's sits in an area at one time deeply decimated by the HIV/AIDS pandemic. It was an ugly era, one where the Church neither condoned nor condemned the negative labeling of the disease as GRID or Gay-Related Immune Deficiency. In a *New York Times* article on November 13, 1989 Cardinal Joseph O'Conner said, "Sometimes I believe the greatest damage done to persons with AIDS is done by the dishonesty of those health care professionals who refuse to confront the moral dimensions of sexual aberrations or drug abuse. Good morality is good medicine." That to me sums up what I term "The Francis Defect", the dishonesty of those moral theologians and gay or straight priests who to confront the positive moral dimensions of same-sex love and same-sex relationships, refuse to examine the disastrous effects of anti-gay theology and anti-gay rhetoric. In this case, bad morality, bad theology is bad medicine.

About midway through my summer job at St. Luke's in the Fields, I met with Mother Melanie Fuller. Since I was no longer Roman Catholic, I sought to learn about reception into the Episcopal Church. As we sat together, she distilled for me the relationship between The Book of Common

Prayer, Episcopal Polity and the Hymnal; listening to her, I felt an incipient attraction to the Episcopal Church. Truth be told, I didn't like being a homeless man, and that's exactly how I felt as a former Jesuit and a former Catholic—homeless. (It pains me to say this, my heart is broken.)

As a Jesuit I was trained in the spirituality of our founder Saint Ignatius of Loyola. For just about ten years, I practiced the discernment of spirits, seeking to know God through the movements of the good spirit and being tempted in my life with God by evil. I felt let down by the Church, asking, "Why is the Church leaving so many behind?"

As I learned more about the Episcopal Church's own mission, I imagined a community of faithful people's continuously evolving through *chronos* and *kairos* time (man's time and God's time) to include, *e.g.*, women who desire ordination, and women who desire the use of contraception, not to have an abortion, to make love without the fear or worry of adding unwanted children to their family. The Episcopal Church's mission is very human, which means it is also complicated and messy, *e.g.*, the elevation of Gene Robinson as an openly gay Bishop.

Yet, I remembered LGBTQ Roman Catholics who were led to the pews of "gay friendly" parishes like St. Francis Xavier, Good Shepherd or St. Cecilia's. These parishes were run by liberal diocesan priests or liberal religious orders like the Jesuits, Paulists and Franciscans OFM. To me the Episcopal Church embodied *en vivo* St. Ignatius' theology of human flourishing. For him, *The Spiritual Exercises* are an exhortatory means for a rather close and personal encounter between Jesus, the Godhead, and the retreatant, the human meeting the Divine in time, one that will fulfill itself not in encounter but in relationship. To me that is what the Episcopal Church offered, relationship not encounter—the capacity to wrestle with issues out in the open, with laity and clerics who agree and disagree, something impossible to imagine within the hierarchy of the Roman Catholic Church.

I meditated on the lives of unmarried or remarried men and women who were spiritually poor, who felt left out because of an overemphasis on the needs of those without food, or shelter, but for whom the Church said, "because you are divorced, you cannot supper at the table of the Lord." Such is the paradox of the papacy of the very green and populist Pope Francis I.

As the African-American intellectual and mentor, Cornel West, says, "Deep integrity must trump cheap popularity. To pursue truth and justice is to live dangerously."

As my first experiences of *The Book of Common Prayer* came to an end I was consoled knowing that God was acting in my life, that the grace of the Holy Spirit was in me. Although during this time I was filled with apprehension, I now felt an influx of peace.

While I felt some loss about my departure from the Society of Jesus, the good spirit, which led me toward consolation, enkindled me, and I felt gratitude deeply, something that the spirituality of the Society of Jesus and the Anglican Communion share.

Today, I do not wrestle with how to be gay and Christian in the Roman Catholic Church. Instead, I actively participate in services in the Episcopal Church, publish articles from time to time, and work with students in public education. I am also completing my doctorate at Teachers College, Columbia University where I examine the possible intersection between the pedagogical philosophy of Saint Ignatius of Loyola and the character formation of public school students. The years since my departure have been mixed with consolation and desolation. That is what it means to be living a pilgiram's journey.

I end my memoir where I began, with gratitude in sharing how I arrived at my true self. Mostly, as I receive and carry out my mission from the Society, to continue being a layperson, I return to the world of dating and to human touch. At the Easter Vigil (2015) as I was received into the Anglican Communion, I remained priestly, but I was no longer studying for the priesthood. I learned again what it meant to be Christian in the city that never sleeps.

The Danish philosopher and theologian, Soren Kierkegaard once wrote, "Life must be lived forwards, but it can only be understood backwards." When I had professed vows on August 11, 2007, I promised to enter the Society of Jesus and to remain within it forever. At the mass, I thought of Earl, who stood in the back of the church. I thought of Fr. John Languish who called me part of a blessed trinity. Then I turned around, and saw my dad, Albert James Brenkert, weeping, tears of joy running down his cheeks. I looked only for an instant, while his silence told me everything: his love for me was bold, courageous, true and eternal.

Then I heard Jesuits starting to sing, *Take, Lord, and receive, all my liberty, my memory, my understanding, and my entire will-all that I have and call my own*, and bewildered by the love poured out on the cross, I stood up and started to sing.

For the next nine years, I'd be missioned around the world as a Jesuit in good standing. Some may call me strident, others might call me foolish or angry, still others will call me an authentic Christian witness. At my reception into the Episcopal Church, the sky did not fall, nor did meteors hit the Hudson River; no, the simple liturgy captured God's time and gave to us all the gift of grace, the gift to be God's in a community.

On June 15, 2014, the feast day of Charles Lwanga and Companions, Martyrs of Uganda, I wrote my Jesuit brothers about my departure from the Society of Jesus. I desired sacramental priesthood, but could not seek priesthood while LGBTQ persons of faith or no faith were being fired or penalized or criminalized because of whom they loved. Priesthood and social justice are part of one call, for some men it can be mystical, but one does not become a priest because he desires to celebrate sacraments alone, Jesus himself is the penultimate sacrifice, the one oblation of the Lord. In Baptism the Christian is incorporated into Christ's body and sent on Christ's mission.

Thus, after a period of prayer and discernment, I wrote the brothers of my small community:

> Dear Brothers of Miguel Pro,
>
> After a year-long discernment, including deep prayer and much consolation I am now freely and actively departing the Society of Jesus.
>
> You have each been a beacon of life for me and a companion on the journey, for this I am grateful.
>
> I have completed my discernment under the direction of my spiritual director, our rector, and close Jesuit and lay friends. Recently I completed an 8-day retreat, in Cambridge, where I was accompanied by Fr. Robert Dowd, during which I sought and received additional confirmation and clarity about my discernment. I wrote my dismissal letter on the feast day of saints Charles Lwanga and Companions, Martyrs of Uganda. Martyrs, who now pray for the LGBTQ men and women physically and spiritually imprisoned by the Church, many of whom live on the continent of Africa, or in countries like Uganda.
>
> Having now met with my Provincial, I leave the Society in good standing, and with great peace and gratitude. I am most happy to speak with you in person, or by phone, to tell you about my discernment and the reasons for my departure.
>
> As a Jesuit my spiritual self and vocation flourished. As the poet Mary Oliver says, "I have been risky in my endeavors, I have been steadfast in my loves; Oh Lord consider these when you judge me. Mine too is a vivid a blessed life, a pilgrim on a marvelous and Spirit-led journey."
>
> With fellow Jesuit Richard Zanoni, S.J. I know that, "Taken separately, we are men of little worth, God knows. But the point about us is that we cannot be taken separately; we must be taken together; and, taken together, we may perhaps count for something in God's plan to save the world." This is *Magis*.
>
> Please be assured of my thoughts and prayers. With great affection and love,
>
> Ben

When I signed the paperwork, sealing my departure from the Jesuits on July 16, 2014, my provincial told me, "Ben, on this issue you are right, but there is nothing the east coast Jesuit provinces can do. In the meantime we are meeting with lawyers to explore employment and volunteer protections for LGBTQ people." How timid!

As a lay person, missioned by the Society of Jesus to the frontiers and margins of the Church, I desire to do what any son of Ignatius might—to pray for the grace from the Second Week of *The Spiritual Exercises*: "to know Jesus more intimately, to love Him more dearly, and to follow Him more closely." Still today, I am living and breathing the Fifth Week of the Spiritual Exercises. I am who I am because of the love that surrounds me, I could not be who I am without that love. I am full of gratitude.

Let me conclude by saying that there are many Jesuit friends that I want to thank by real name, but cannot. These Jesuit friends had such a profound, dynamic, and kerygmatic affect on my life. It is hard and painful to say why my former brothers feel deeply alienated from me; it is unclear to me why they feel let down by my departure, or about the veracity of my narrative. Perhaps they feel vulnerable, which I must respect. I love them.

Yet, these men were my companions on a journey; brothers who served side-by-side with me, as much as any family member or best friend might. In paying tribute to them, and their impact on my life, I reveal a deep longing for those Jesuit friendships. But mostly, I acknowledge that there has not been a day that has gone by, since my departure, when I have not prayed for them. I very much hoped that I could answer this question from my prayer, Will everything work towards the good in the long run? Life is long, and I have no crystal ball, magic wand or genie-in-a-bottle, how life unfolds I cannot know. I do have a heart full of love, and when I remember these three Jesuit friends my heart fills with gratitude for them.

I would like to write about them but I can't. They will always be in my heart.

All for the Greater Glory of God, *Ad Majorem Dei Gloriam.*

Epilogue

An Incoherent Truth

As I write this epilogue, in 2020 during the days of the COVID-19 lockdown and the Black Lives Matter protests I pray for a world where all LGBTQ people flourish as individuals and as members of their faith community. But religious life and sacramental priesthood are not an option for most Catholics, especially for those who are annoyed or frustrated with the Church's homophobia and discrimination against LGBTQ people. Society-at-large is growing less tolerant of the latter, *e.g.*, consider how the world is embracing the story of the transgender heroine Caitlyn Jenner (aka the American Olympic gold medalist Bruce Jenner). Still, Pope Francis I warns against gender theory, which he calls ideological colonization. Consider the disparity between stories about LGBTQ people being fired from Church institutions and stories about the positive contributions, including the spiritual formation of youth and adults by LGBTQ people. Can any news reporter ensure that married LGBTQ employees will "have" their job after a story is published?

In April 2015, I learned about the public coming out of a younger Jesuit, one fresh from the Novitiate, who was studying in Chicago. Apparently, his superiors supported him. Were my superiors too timid, or uncaring or oblivious? I was deeply hurt, and felt betrayed. This could have been my story.

Time does not stand still, all of which brings me to May 2015, when, of all Catholic nations, the Irish voted to approve same-sex marriage! Then in June 2015 the United States Supreme Court ruled in favor of gay marriage in the case *Obergefell v. Hodges*. Ireland and America's historic approval of same-sex marriage is a major milestone for LGBTQ rights and a recognition of equality. Of course, what is legal doesn't always conform to the Roman Catholic Church's doctrine. American prelates like Archbishops Salvatore Cordileone, Charles Chaput and John Myers, and Cardinals Timothy Dolan and Sean O'Malley have remained mostly silent on the issue, refusing to offer comment or to give interviews; the Church's youth have moved on without the Church's blessing. They demand that their Church become the Holy Mother she claims to be—they want Holy Mother Church to publicly recognize their friends, family members and colleagues. These youth ask, Can one pope's smile outlive doctrine, dogma or the tradition? These youth ask, How does a Church treat people with the fullness of Christ's dignity when she must condemn their intimacy and same-sex attraction as "disordered" and "morally evil" or "inconsistent with nature"?

In Ireland, the United States of America, even Costa Rica and around the world, the Church can no longer deny that homosexuality exists in nature. While Bishops like Kevin Doran tell the world that homosexuality, like down syndrome, (an absurd analogy) is not part of God's plan, the Church in the pews moves forward. Moreover, the Church cannot deny that many of her priests and religious are gay men, who might have sought the priesthood because the Church teaches that they are "intrinsically disordered" or that forced celibacy was the only option for a "true" life in Christ.

In the wake of the vote in Ireland and the U.S. Supreme Court decision, the Catholic Church meets the bevy of articles and news reports by ignoring the popular vote with mixed intrigue, still the Pope's second in command commented about the Irish vote, "I was very saddened by this result...I don't think we can speak only about a defeat for Christian principles, but a defeat for humanity." Consider how from retirement Pope Emeritus Benedict XVI walks back the progress of Pope Francis I. It is as if Pope Benedict is telling Pope Francis: Thank you my Brother in Christ. I respect your sincerity, but I firmly believe the teaching of Scripture and the Church on these matters. I do understand the honesty of your convictions; I'm sure you will respect the strength of mine. It was unfortunate when the movie, The Two Popes portrayed Pope Benedict weakly, and Pope Francis headstrong, for Benedict erodes any possibility of progress.

The Church is not listening to her people, the culture wars continue! After the Orlando Gay Massacre Pope Francis and other Church leaders prayed away the gay, praying for the conversion of souls is easy, naming the dead, identifying them as gay Christians hard. It matters that they were LGBTQ because they were killed because they were LGBTQ. Actions speak louder than words. To date the Church has not held a mass for gays at the Vatican or anywhere in the world: No action. The Church cannot get away with practicing sexuality-blindness.

Merriam-Webster defines Incoherent, an adjective, as lacking coherence, cohesion; lacking orderly continuity, arrangement or relevance and lacking normal clarity or intelligibility in speech or thought. Pope Francis' comments are inconsistent with the Church's catechism, doctrine, dogma and tradition. Pope Francis' loose speak generates mixed messages and smoke signals; his public statements are often illogical and disorganized (Is he just telling people what they want to hear?), and the media love to write about him because he sells papers and magazines. While Pope Francis may see himself as easily understood or expressing himself in simple ways for the general public, to me he sounds more and more like a politician.

As a Cardinal in Argentina Pope Francis I (Jorge Cardinal Bergoglio) once told listeners that our Church has at times become too insular, leading to spiritual sickness, that we must avoid a "Church [that] remains closed in on itself, self-referential, [one that] gets old."

To this I respond with a question posed to me by my last Jesuit Provincial, whom I admire and love: *What is the Society of Jesus doing today that would or could cause her to be suppressed (again)?*

In 1773, the Society of Jesus was suppressed just as the world faced the introduction of modernity, secularism and the end of the *ancien regime*. In 2020, which openly or closeted gay Jesuit will speak prophetically for the rights of the LGBTQ community? Do modern Jesuits have the courage of their forbears? Or will the Church make sure they remain silent (and suppressed)?

As for me, I cannot abide being a part of an institution that fires even one gay or lesbian for being openly gay or for being married to the person they love. The Jesuit motto that I still love so much is a part of my being, and as a gay man I remain full of gratitude knowing that I embarked upon writing this book for many reasons and one of them is: *All for the Greater Glory of God.* Amen.

Yes, I remained a Jesuit for nearly ten years, a member in good standing until my departure in 2014. I count my time as a postulant amongst Jesuits as good and generous years. I made some wonderful friends, met many Jesuit heroes and mentors, visited extraordinary places; it was a time when I tried to live as authentically as possible the voluntary vows of poverty, chastity and obedience. That was just it: voluntary, but *mandatory*. Since the 11th Century, the Roman Catholic Church had implemented voluntary but mandatory celibacy, which was promised by diocesan priests and vowed by religious men and women. Whether one was gay or straight, they had to live celibately.

Overtime I've read salient texts like, Fr. Donald Goergen, O.P.'s *The Sexual Celibate*, Keith Clark's *Being Sexual and Celibate*, and Fr. Sonny Manuel, S.J.'s *Living Celibacy: Healthy Pathways for Priests*. With each text, the rationale for the discipline seemed less important to the means of making it work. The Church posited that her priests and religious could serve more freely without a partner, that their spouse is the Church, that they are the bridegrooms of Jesus Christ. My memory tells me that some lived happier celibate lives than others. While I continued to practice celibacy, I learned about the privileging of gay priests, that Holy Orders gave some gay men an advantage over and above many, many other LGBTQ people who desired to marry a person of the same gender.

As I stopped drinking, and took on greater sobriety, I received help from others who stopped drinking. With other sober gay friends, I became aware (*sic* reborn) of the truth that the Church is becoming increasingly hostile toward the LGBTQ community. Whether or not it was through the final years of Saint John Paul II or the papacy of Pope Emeritus Benedict XVI or now in the era of the *Francis Effect* and *Who am I to judge?*, the Church remains at odds with the reality of pastoral care at gay-friendly parishes like St. Francis Xavier in New York City. It is Pope Francis who speaks so eloquently about the environment, but who warns against reverting to individualism in response to the COVID-19 pandemic. If the Church offers only a bridge to dialogue as an olive branch to LGBTQ people: Can a LGBTQ person seek communion in a Church that denies them full membership, including reception of the Eucharist?

Still today, the Church's official teaching on homosexuality contributes to the homelessness of some 400,000 LGBTQ youth in the United States alone. Still today outing people, especially gay priests, poses such a threat to people's livelihoods that such actions are considered destructive.

Being gay is not negative. Gays, especially gay children and teenagers do not need to exhale for being gay, such is the misnomer captured by the popular gay coming of age film, *Love, Simon* (2018). Being gay is positive, life and God affirming. Outing people confronts social sin, structural evil and systemic harm caused by, *e.g.*, the millennia of anti-gay rhetoric and theology espoused by the Roman Catholic Church. Outing Roman Catholic gay priests confronts their *acedia* (state of listlessness or torpor) from which they deny their privilege, condition or even their existential and ontological identity as men who serve *in persona Christi*. These are the very men who should have been the first to come out, but they remain the last. That has not been the charge of this memoir. *It has been to be helpful and hopeful of change, to offer through my personal narrative another way for LGBTQ Christians to participate in communal religion: to courage to leave the Church of the their youth, their current life for another that is fully LGBTQ affirming.*

In future books, I hope to address such an egregious hypocrisy: When gay priests teach against homosexuality, they create the added problem of gay men who hate themselves and live under the guise that they are straight (unless they've told other priests in the same situation) because no one knows they are gay. Should we pity such people? I think not. If they are that self-loathing, they should not be teaching young people about the catechism, dogma, doctrine and tradition of the Church.

How will the Roman Catholic Church respond to the June 15, 2020 ruling by the United States Supreme Court: Federal civil rights law protects LGBTQ workers under Title VII of the Civil Rights Act? The 6-3 ruling was written by Justice Neil Gorsuch, a Trump appointee and Chief Justice John Roberts. Justice Gorsuch wrote in the majority opinion that, "In Title VII, Congress adopted broad language making it illegal for an employer to rely on an employee's sex when deciding to fire that employee . . . We do not hesitate to recognize today a necessary consequence of that legislative choice: An employer who fires an individual merely for being gay or transgender defies the law." It remains to be seen: Will the Roman Catholic Church, her diocesan and religious order sponsored churches and schools rehire the workers and volunteers they terminated from employment and volunteer activities like Colleen Simon and Nicholas Coppola?

Perhaps when these churches and other religious institutions do discriminate (and those that have already) based on sexual orientation and gender identity they will and should lose their non-profit status because now it is the law of the land.

My memoir, *A Catechism of the Heart: A Jesuit Missioned to the Laity*, challenges society to confront injustice and social sin; it also employs the lenses of theology, philosophy and social work to address what potential change can look like. My memoir underscores the reasons why I left the Jesuits, and how I obediently accepted my religious superiors' missioning me back to the laity. Other gay Jesuits may follow their religious superiors orders to remain closeted differently, perhaps they can because their life is comfortable, perhaps they do so because they are full of conviction, that like me, in following their vow of obedience, one is more available to the Society of Jesus and to the Church. Why does being gay limit a gay priest's availability? Simply put, it shouldn't. It takes courage and conviction to be out publicly as a gay man, especially as a gay priest: one cannot be afraid of one's own shadow. Surely, being a closeted gay priest is less helpful than being an openly gay priest: In 2020, who is the better role model for gay young people living throughout America's cities, suburbs, towns and rural areas?

To catechize is to teach by word of mouth. A kind of teaching that demands question and answer. To question searchingly. Thus, to have a catechism of the heart is to have a heart that teaches and searches for the truth. Thus, my memoir searched for truth: Self-truth, Church-truth, Jesuit-truth, and World-truth. In my memoir, readers met the Spirituality of Saint Ignatius of Loyola, the Basque nobleman who founded the Society of Jesus (the Jesuits) in 1540, and whose *Spiritual Exercises* and rules for the discernment of spirits helped me to trust God's calling. St. Ignatius' motto is *Ad Majorem Dei Gloriam*, for the greater Glory of God, meaning to give to God glory, and to direct all of one's actions to that end. In my memoir readers encountered some gay sex scenes; these scenes are not used to test the merits and virtues of prudish-minded people, but rather to limit the prevailing effects of homophobia, to universalize same-sex desire and same-sex as parts of the spectrum of sex and sexuality. I invoked reader's patience with those few scenes.

Why do gay men enter the Roman Catholic priesthood? They believe in God's love, and they believe God calls them to become priests. They have an absolute conviction that God has called them to the priesthood of all believers. Some of these men choose the actual poverty of the Franciscans, the preaching order of the Dominicans, the missionary and independent life of the Maryknolls or the model of St. Paul in the Paulist Fathers. Gay men are called to be priests in orders for whom their founder's charism attracts them. These are not theological differences, but rather differences in style of vocation, mission or apostolic work, and the way a community lives together. A Jesuit is very different from a Benedictine, a Franciscan friar is very different from a Trappist monk. Some call Jesuits egotistical, Franciscans aloof, and Dominicans terrible preachers.

For St. Ignatius of Loyola, memory, understanding and will are key means through which one forms his or her Christian identity, which hopefully leads to a life of perfect charity. Yes, leaving priestly formation was painful; it left me feeling empty and angry. Narrating my story honestly was important to my grief and bereavement and ultimately my healing. I still hope to be ordained an openly gay priest, one that can now marry and have a family. But that will happen in God's time, if God desires it for me in this lifetime. I end my memoir (*sic* confession) with gratitude, a vitally important characteristic of Ignatian Spirituality, and I ask for the grace that readers may be able to discover themselves in my story, that our time together may prove fruitful, emerging in increased compassion and human flourishing.

I offer St. Ignatius' Prayer for Generosity as a means to end our companionship:

> Lord, teach me to be generous.
> Teach me to serve you as you deserve;
> to give and not to count the cost,
> to fight and not to heed the wounds,
> to toil and not to seek for rest,
> to labor and not to ask for reward,
> save that of knowing that I do your will.

Made in the USA
Middletown, DE
21 October 2023

41146077R00096